T0105858

# REPORT WRITING

# FOR

# POLICE OFFICERS

(2nd ed.)

$$(\exists x)P(x) \neq (\forall x)P(x)$$

$$P \Rightarrow Q \neq Q \Rightarrow P$$

by

Wayne L. Davis, Ph.D.

Copyright © 2013 Wayne L. Davis, Ph.D.

All rights reserved. No part of this book may be used or reproduced by any means, graphic, electronic, or mechanical, including photocopying, recording, taping or by any information storage retrieval system without the written permission of the publisher except in the case of brief quotations embodied in critical articles and reviews.

Balboa Press books may be ordered through booksellers or by contacting:

Balboa Press
A Division of Hay House
1663 Liberty Drive
Bloomington, IN 47403
www.balboapress.com
1 (877) 407-4847

Because of the dynamic nature of the Internet, any web addresses or links contained in this book may have changed since publication and may no longer be valid. The views expressed in this work are solely those of the author and do not necessarily reflect the views of the publisher, and the publisher hereby disclaims any responsibility for them.

The author of this book does not dispense medical advice or prescribe the use of any technique as a form of treatment for physical, emotional, or medical problems without the advice of a physician, either directly or indirectly. The intent of the author is only to offer information of a general nature to help you in your quest for emotional and spiritual well-being. In the event you use any of the information in this book for yourself, which is your constitutional right, the author and the publisher assume no responsibility for your actions.

Any people depicted in stock imagery provided by Thinkstock are models, and such images are being used for illustrative purposes only. Certain stock imagery © Thinkstock.

ISBN: 978-1-4525-8726-4 (sc)
ISBN: 978-1-4525-8725-7 (e)

Library of Congress Control Number: 2013920726

Printed in the United States of America.

Balboa Press rev. date: 11/19/2013

BALBOA.
PRESS
A DIVISION OF HAY HOUSE

# Preface

This book is designed for criminal justice instructors. This book requires the instructors to help students work through the various police reports. The reports are intentionally left incomplete and they require students to work through them. Some reports may seem to ask confusing questions, which may lead to unreliable responses. This is to be used as a learning lesson: responses that are not reliable create statistics that are not valid. Managers need to improve the forms in order to obtain valid data.

This book first discusses communication theory and how it applies to police officers and prosecutors in the courtroom. Information presented in the courtroom by police officers has a significant impact upon the jurors. Indeed, police officers communicate both verbally and nonverbally in the courtroom and this affects their credibility on the stand. Furthermore, by employing persuasion theories, prosecutors can align the officers' testimonies to the jurors' particular communication preference. Second, this book discusses truth as it relates to probable cause and beyond a reasonable doubt. Finally, because report writing is a significant part of police work, this book presents a variety of police forms that will engage students in written communication.

Wayne L. Davis, Ph.D.

Wayne L. Davis holds a Bachelor of Science in Electrical Engineering from the University of Michigan-Dearborn, a Master of Science in Business Administration from Madonna University in Livonia, Michigan, and a Ph.D. in Criminal Justice from Capella University in Minneapolis, Minnesota. In addition, Dr. Davis has earned a helicopter pilot license, an advanced open water scuba diver certification, a technician plus amateur radio license (N8ZFG), and a basic emergency medical technician certificate from the State of Michigan.

Dr. Davis has graduated from three different law enforcement academies (city, state, and federal): Schoolcraft College in Livonia, Michigan, the Indiana Law Enforcement Law Academy, and the Federal Law Enforcement Training Center. He has over 20 years of law enforcement experience with city, state, and federal law enforcement agencies.

While he worked as a product design engineer at Ford Motor Company, Dr. Davis introduced the electronic engine control module into the pleasure boat industry. This included writing a product specification manual and performing test-to-failure statistical research. As a result, Dr. Davis was nominated for the Ford Motor Company Electronics Division Worldwide Leadership Excellence Award. Subsequently, this led to his research paper called, *A Study of Factors Affecting a Supply Decision by the Ford Motor Company International Division for Original Equipment.*

Dr. Davis has received numerous awards and publications. Dr. Davis has received the U.S. Customs & Border Protection Commissioner's Award, the U.S. Customs & Border Protection Scholastic Award, and he was appointed to a field-training officer by the Indiana State Police. In addition, Dr. Davis has conducted an exploratory research study called, *A Correlational Study of Childhood Religiosity, Childhood Sport Participation, and Sport-Learned Aggression among African American Female Athletes.* Subsequently, Dr. Davis has published several textbooks, which include a) *Critical Thinking: Totality of Circumstances,* b) *Police-Community Relations: Different Lenses & Perception of Truth,* c) *Interviewing, Interrogation, and Communication for Law Enforcement,* and d) *Terrorism, Homeland Security, and Risk Assessment through Research Proposal.*

Recently, Dr. Davis has created table top police scenes for which he has filed a patent. In addition, he has served as the Academic Coordinator for the Criminal Justice and Human Services Programs at Aiken Technical College in Aiken, SC. With the support of local law enforcement agencies, Dr. Davis has created an application-based criminal justice program that meets the needs of the local community.

# Table of Contents

## List of Tables

# List of Figures

# POLICE REPORTS WITHIN THIS TEXTBOOK

# INCIDENT REPORTS (NON-CRIMINAL) ...................... 108

# CRIMINAL & JUVENILE REPORTS ............................... 122

# CHAPTER 1.  COMMUNICATION THEORY

## Introduction – The Need to Communicate

Although the U.S. has less than 5% of the world's population, it has nearly 25% of the world's total prison population (Liptak, 2008). Having such a large incarceration rate is due, in part, to get tough policies and longer prison sentences (Kelley, Mueller, & Hemmens, 2004). Indeed, at the end of 2007 in the U.S., there were about 2.3 million people incarcerated, 4.2 million people on probation, and 800,000 people on parole (Fears, 2008; McCarthy, 2009). Hence, there is a need for police reports.

Since September 2001, federal resources, which were previously used to fund local law enforcement, have been redirected toward homeland security (Kingsbury, 2006).  With a 45% cut in funds, many local law enforcement agencies have reduced their manpower. Some midsize cities have reduced their manpower by about 25%.  In addition, according to Kingsbury, U.S. prisons are releasing about 630,000 inmates each year and the recidivism rate from state prisons is about 67%.  Thus, with fewer police officers on the streets and more criminals on the streets, there is a public safety concern.

From 2011 to 2012, the FBI has indicated that there was an increase in the number of violent crimes in the U.S. (Federal Bureau of Investigation, 2013).  In 2012, the FBI has indicated that there were more than 1.2 million violent crimes, such as murder, robberies, and aggravated assaults.  As the number of crimes increase, more arrests will be made. Therefore, police officers can expect to find themselves in the courtroom more often. Indeed, the public's safety depends upon prosecutors and police officers performing effectively within the courtroom.

To effectively serve the public, a police officer must be a credible witness in the courtroom during a trial.  Part of the job of a police officer is to arrest criminals, to complete the proper paperwork, and then to testify in the courtroom.  Poor paperwork may indicate in court that the oficer is lazy or incompetent.  Officers who fail to write effectively have failed to do their jobs and have failed to adequately protect the public. In short, police officers must learn how to properly testify in court and to effectively persuade jurors.

For example, if a defense attorney discovers mistakes in a police report, the defense attorney may ask the officer if the officer has performed the work to the best of his or her ability. At this point, the officer is in trouble because the officer must admit that he or she is incompetent or deceitful (if best effort was put forward) or that he or she is lazy and sloppy (if best effort was not put forward).

## History of Communication and Persuasion Theories

Communication theory as it relates to persuasion theory started around the 5th century BCE (Schiappa, 1991). During this time, Protagoras (490-421 BCE), a philosophical thinker in Athens, became the pioneer of the study of language; he invented a new way of thinking and speaking. Protagoras, the father of debate and a promoter of democracy, organized dialogue and invented the lecture between teachers and students. Each side presented an argument in an informal discussion group and then had to defend it. About the same time, in 466 BCE, the Sicilian government was overthrown. That government, consequently, changed from tyranny to democracy. As a result, there was a high demand for people to be able to speak their minds in assemblies and to be able to testify for themselves in court. There were few lawyers at that time. Meeting this demand, Corax and Tisias, two Sicilians, developed the argument from probability. Thus, persuasive arguments had begun.

In 1776, the American Revolution took place. During this era, the U.S. Constitution was written, which affords each person charged with a crime the right to a trial by jury. Like Great Britain, trials are based on an adversarial model, where debate is expected (Resnick & Knoll, 2007). Thus, the founding fathers have promoted communication theory and persuasive arguments within the courtroom; it has always been a part of U.S. history.

In modern times, there have been several landmark theories involving communication theory and interpersonal persuasion (Reardon, 1981). These landmark theories include: 1) the Balance Theory; 2) the Attribution Theory; 3) Congruity Principle Theory; 4) the Cognitive Dissonance Theory; 5) the Learning Theory; 6) the Functional Theory; 7) the Inoculation Theory; and 8) the CounterAttitudinal Advocacy Theory. Indeed, communication theory is a very broad field of study (Stremler, 1982).

During the 1950s, Fritz Heider developed the Balance Theory (Crandall, Silvia, N'Gbala, Tsang, & Dawson, 2007; Reardon, 1981). This theory states that people like consistency and they resist change. Because people like to remain static, successful persuasion must create a degree of imbalance from the status quo. In addition, Heider also developed the Attribution Theory, which states that people seek reasons to justify someone else's behavior. This is the reason to seek a motive when a person commits a crime.

Also during the 1950s, Osgood and Tannenbaum developed the Congruity Principle Theory (Reardon, 1981). This states that when a person is confronted with two or more incompatible concepts, the person will change his or her attitude so that the two concepts are congruent. For example, if John supports the death penalty and his friend Lisa does not, then every time John thinks of Lisa he will have negative feelings toward her due to her stance on the death penalty.

In 1957, Leon Festinger developed the Cognitive Dissonance Theory (Reardon, 1981). This theory states that two relations, dissonant and consonant, are associated with cognitive elements. Dissonant relations between two cognitive elements produce negative feelings; thus, people behave in ways that reduce dissonance. An example of a dissonant relation between two elements would be a person going into debt when buying a house (this is stressful). On the other hand, consonant relations imply an appropriate match of two cognitive elements, such as not buying a home because one is already in debt.

During the 1960s, Staats developed the Learning Theory, which describes how people are conditioned to respond in particular ways (Reardon, 1981). People can be trained to provide certain responses based on certain information provided to them. A classic example of conditioning would be the experiment when Pavlov conditioned a dog to saliva at the sound of a bell. Also during the 1960s, Katz developed the Functional Theory. According to the Functional Theory, people tend to behave and perform only those actions that they find favorable, they refuse to humble themselves and admit their faults, they act in ways to foster preferred impressions, and they tend to act in ways that provide certainty. Continuing with the 1960s, according to Reardon, McGuire developed the Inoculation Theory. This theory states that the best persuasion is one that supports one side of an argument and, at the same time, refutes the other side of the argument. By explaining both the benefits for doing something and costs for doing something else, this will be more persuasive; it is like being pushed and pulled in the same direction. Furthermore, by reinforcing the message with multiple sources, this will improve credibility and, thus, be more persuasive (Tucker, Donovan, & Marlatt, 1999).

During the 1970s, Miller and Burgoon developed the CounterAttitudinal Advocacy Theory (Reardon, 1981). This theory states that people will best construe their own beliefs and behaviors when rewards are not associated with their activities. This theory is the opposite of the theory based on incentives, which states that people will perform those acts that are rewarded.

## Communication Theory

U.S. democratic principles rely upon truth being discovered through open debates within the courtroom (Bank, 2001). Therefore, communication theory is critical in law enforcement, especially within the courtroom. Indeed, the way police officers communicate within the courtroom will influence the jurors' decisions. The basic assumptions of communication theory indicate that jurors perceive information that impacts their attitudes, resulting in decisions that could be significant (Tucker et al., 1999). For example, based on the information that they receive and perceive, the jurors may set a killer loose, or, on the

4

other hand, they may convict an innocent person. Thus, prosecutors and police officers, who are the message sources, use persuasion to affect the attitudes and opinions of the jurors in order to arrive at an appropriate verdict (Tucker et al.). Although most police officers receive very little training in courtroom testimony, the jurors believe otherwise and have high expectations for them (Smith & Hilderbrand, n.d.). Thus, the jurors already have a misconception about how well the police officers should testify. Consequently, police officers must learn how to effectively communicate in the courtroom so that their testimonies are credible. In short, persuasion is directly related to credibility.

*Verbal Persuasion*

A police officer's verbal communication in the courtroom impacts the police officer's credibility as a witness. Verbal communication can be either written or spoken. If it is written, then it takes the form of police reports, which may include arrest reports. If it is vocal, then it takes the form of oral testimony. Indeed, both types of verbal communication impact the office's credibility as a witness. In all cases, any communication that is less than truthful is illegal and unacceptable. This being said, it is assumed that the police officers have made justifiable arrests in which they are testifying.

A police officer's written report is a reflection of the police officer's competence. First of all, a police report must have good content, and the officer must be familiar with its content (Speaking, 2006). Because it is not uncommon for a trial to take place years after the arrest, the police officer should review the report prior to the trial. In other words, a police officer should never go to the stand without knowing what is in his or her report. Otherwise, the defense attorney will make the officer look like a fool, and this is not the image that the officer wants to portray to the jury. Furthermore, the police report must contain all pertinent information; if it is not written down in the report, then it cannot be used in court (Stewart, 2007). In other words, there is no pulling a rabbit out of a magic hat. Second, the report must be objective, complete, accurate, and clear. For example, if a hockey team played 10 games and is undefeated, this does not mean that the team has won ten games; they could have tied some of them. Misleading the jury is unethical, and an officer must present a true representation of the facts. In addition, the police officer should use active statements instead of passive statements. This can be achieved by focusing on what witnesses saw, rather than by focusing on what witnesses did not see. For instance, the statements, *"I did not see the driver look back before he backed his car,"* is not equivalent to, *"I saw the driver not look back before he backed his car."* The former statement is problematic because it may indicate that the witness saw nothing, but the latter statement is valuable and describes what the witness actually saw. Third, in order to keep the jury's attention, the report must be organized and structured. It is just like watching television; in order to keep the jurors interested and to help them understand the flow of events, the report must not keep changing channels/directions (Boccaccini, 2002). The report should flow smoothly, and this requires proper grammar. If there are grammar mistakes within the report, the jurors will perceive the officer as either lazy and uncaring or incompetent. If the officer is perceived as unprofessional, uncaring, or incompetent, then the jurors may transfer that negative perception to the validity of the report. In the jurors' minds, if they believe that the officer is a fool, then they will consider themselves bigger fools if they agree. Finally, because defense attorneys are experts at finding weaknesses in police officers' reports, police officers must put the necessary time and effort into writing good reports. Indeed, their credibility will be determined by the evidence presented in the courtroom, which is their written documentations (Lewis, 2001).

A police officer's oral testimony is a reflection of the police officer's competence. Testifying on the stand can be intimidating and can cause anxiety, but police officers must maintain their professionalism and objectivity (Klimon, 1985). When testifying, it is more important to make a lasting impression rather than to present a perfect testimony (Maxey & O'Connor, 2007). Specifically, if an officer makes a mistake or cannot remember a particular event, the officer must admit it as soon as it is realized (Lewis, 2001; Reynolds, 1990). The jurors understand that no one is perfect and that people make mistakes. By a police officer admitting a mistake right away, the jurors will perceive that particular officer as human and honest, rather than one who is trying to cover things up.

When police officers are testifying in court, they should never start a sentence with, *"To be honest"* or *"To tell the truth,"* because this will give the impression to the jurors

6

that the rest of the testimony is less than truthful (Being, 2001). In addition, if the truth is to be discovered, the officers must persuade the jurors using plain language (Lewis, 2001; Navarro, 2004; Stewart, 2007). If a police officer uses slang or police jargon, then the jurors may either become confused, not understanding what is being said, or they may perceive that the officer is insulting them, by trying to make them feel dumb and inferior. Both cases will impede persuasion. For example, suppose an officer said, *"District 11, 11-43, 10-23, 7 south, signal 6."* Although this meaning may be quite clear to a police officer in District 11, this is meaningless to the average civilian or juror. As indicated, the officer must present the information in a normal conversational manner.

Testifying in the courtroom is an art and the police officer is a performer (Navarro, 2004). A good way to think about this is to consider the courtroom as an amusement park and the jurors as customers who love thrills. If the police officer rehearses and memorizes the testimony, the jurors will perceive the testimony as a boring and lame merry-go-round (Boccaccini, 2002). Also, if an officer continually pauses during the testimony, jurors will perceive this as a frustrating Ferris wheel, which keeps stopping every few seconds (Navarro). However, by speaking moderately fast with variations in pitch and volume, the jurors will perceive this as a roller coaster, something interesting and exciting. Moreover, the officers must project their voices with confidence, like a big screen television. This will eliminate any perception of doubt in their voices (Defoe, 2007). In short, just as in written communications, weaknesses in a police officer's oral testimony will be exposed. Thus, police officers must practice on being perceived as credible witnesses.

### Nonverbal Persuasion

In addition to communicating verbally, police officers also communicate in many nonverbal, non-symbolic manners (Carter, 2002). Indeed, similar to verbal communication, nonverbal communication in the courtroom also impacts the police officer's credibility as a witness. First of all, a police officer's appearance sets the stage for the perception of his or her credibility as a witness. Because jurors make judgments on the outward appearances of police officers, the officers must dress appropriately and professionally (Navarro, 2004; Stewart, 2007). The jurors may make the analogy that a dirty yard equals a dirty house. In

7

other words, if the officers do not even care enough to take care of themselves, then they probably also do not care about their work. Second, a police officer's conduct impacts the police officer's credibility as a witness. Indeed, police officers must have postures that show interest (Boccaccini, 2002; Lambert, 2008; Navarro). For instance, if a boy is interested in a girl and is about to kiss her, he learns forward toward her and he focuses his eyes upon her. This is an example of a person showing interest, and it is obvious when it is observed. On the other hand, negative body language, such as fidgeting, crossing the arms, looking at one's watch, and looking at the ceiling, gives the impression that the officer has more important things to do than to be in court (Navarro; Tower, 2011). Thus, if the officers are perceived as being disinterested, the jurors will perceive the officers as less than sincere.

### *Implementing Communication Theories within the Courtroom*

Because, according to the **Balance Theory**, people like consistency and they resist change, people must be motivated to change (Reardon, 1981). In this case, a prosecutor can achieve persuasion by distancing the criminal from the jurors. For example, if a person was being tried for public intoxication, the jurors may be strongly resistant to convict the person. The jurors may feel that they have consumed too much alcohol, at one time or another, and that this could be one of them on the stand. However, to overcome this perception, the prosecutor must differentiate the criminal from the jurors. First of all, by drawing a target with concentric circles around it, the prosecutor could start at the outer most ring and state that this level represents the subject's bloodshot eyes. Second, the prosecutor could move to the next circle inward, which represents a person with bloodshot eyes and slurred speech. Third, the prosecutor could move to the next circle inward, which represents bloodshot eyes, slurred speech, and staggering. Fourth, the prosecutor could move to the next circle inward, which represents all of the previous symptoms plus the subject urinating upon the roadway. This continues onward until the center of the target is reached. In this way, the jurors can clearly distance themselves from the defendant and this may persuade them to change their attitudes.

The **Attribution Theory** states that people seek reasons to justify someone else's behavior; they try to find a motive when a person commits a crime (Reardon, 1981).

Suppose a person commits a benevolent act but it is perceived by someone else to be a criminal act, then the motive may be the determining factor for whether a crime has been committed. Because the jurors do not want to convict an innocent person of a crime, and because they do not want themselves to be wrongly convicted of a crime, they desire to find reasons for the actions. Thus, with no motive for committing a crime, the jurors will be less likely to convict a person. As part of the criminal investigation, it is the police officer's job to determine a motive. Once the motive is determined, it is included as part of the written case report. It is then up to the police officer to explain the motive, in simple language, to the jurors so that they will understand it.

The **Congruity Principle Theory** states that jurors will try to align two or more incompatible concepts (Reardon, 1981). The prosecutor and police officer can take advantage of this by aligning the criminal activity to a negative concept held by the jurors. For example, if the local county is dry and the jurors disapprove of alcoholic beverages, then a person who is being tried for possession of marijuana can be associated with being an alcoholic. In this case, the prosecutor can say that marijuana causes intoxication and leads to car crashes, killing innocent people. Furthermore, marijuana is an addictive habit, just like alcohol.

The **Cognitive Dissonance Theory** states that people behave in ways that reduce dissonance between two cognitive elements (Reardon, 1981). In this case, the prosecutor can associate the idea that if the defendant is set free, then one of the jurors may be the defendant's next victim. This stressful perception will persuade the jurors to convict the accused; they will associate the defendant's freedom to negative feelings. Furthermore, by persuading the jurors that justice and democracy demand fair payment for the defendant's actions, and that jail is the perfect place for the accused, the jurors will appropriately match the two cognitive elements.

The **Learning Theory** describes how people are conditioned to respond in particular ways (Reardon, 1981). The county prosecutor is an elected official and knows the local community issues. By associating the particular crime to something that the jurors, who are

9

local community members, find upsetting, the prosecutor can direct their anger toward the accused. For example, if the jurors are upset about paying higher taxes, the prosecutor can illustrate how the accused could not care less about their money problems, as is evidenced by the commission of the criminal act, and that the accused is now mocking them by using their tax paying dollars to get away with it.

According to the **Functional Theory**, people refuse to humble themselves and tend to perform only those actions that they find favorable (Reardon, 1981). In this case, the prosecutor can use the jurors' pride against them by linking the conviction of the accused to the jurors' intelligence. This can be achieved by indicating to the jurors that they are too smart to be fooled by a common criminal (who was not too smart to get caught). By stating that the jurors are community pillars whom the local residents are relying upon to protect them, the jurors may find it beneficial to convict the accused.

The **Inoculation Theory** states that the best persuasion is one that supports one side of an argument and, at the same time, refutes the other side of the argument (Reardon, 1981). In this case, the prosecutor can argue that in order to reduce crime, the accused needs to be locked up. On the other hand, if the jurors fail to convict, their safety is at risk. Thus, the jurors can reduce crime and promote safety at the same time. In order to reinforce this argument and to make it as persuasive as possible, all submitted evidence related to the crime should be emphasized, including victim statements, witness statements, photographs, and laboratory reports (Tucker et al., 1999).

Finally, the **CounterAttitudinal Advocacy Theory** states that people will best construe their own beliefs and behaviors when rewards are not associated with their activities (Reardon, 1981). In this case, the prosecutor can remind the jurors that by serving on the jury, they are serving their community. Convicting the perpetrator is not for personal gain, but it is their patriotic duty as U.S. citizens. Democracy and freedom depend upon law and order. For without law and order, there can be no democracy.

### Conclusion

As mentioned earlier, democracy and truth rely upon open debate within the courtroom (Bank, 2001). However, jurors select their own truths based on their perceptions of the credibility of the information that they receive (Peterson, 1954). One way that this credibility is determined is through the jurors' assessment of the way police officers communicate, both verbally and nonverbally. Thus, police officers must communicate well, be credible, and learn to effectively persuade. A second way that credibility is determined is by the way a prosecutor presents information in the courtroom. By using multiple communication theories, and simultaneously employing as many of them as possible, prosecutors can align information in ways that will be well received by the jurors. Being well received, the information will be more credible. Being more credible, the information will be more persuasive. In short, persuasion through communication is the basic concept of courtroom testimony for both police officers and prosecutors.

# CHAPTER 2.  TRUTH

Quantitative investigations are scientific, objective, and effective in describing phenomena in terms of magnitude (Leedy & Ormrod, 2005).  Quantitative investigations use numeric values and statistics to identify patterns, to objectively quantify relationships between variables, and to make predictions.  Also, because large sample sizes are used, data can be generalized to larger populations.  However, numeric values are ineffective in describing the subjective interpretations of human emotions (Wakefield, 1995).  Because individuals have unique lived experiences and their realities are based on their own perceptions, a single objective truth is unattainable (Hatch, 2002; Weber, 2004).  Indeed, there are multiple realities when dealing with perceptions.  Thus, quantitative investigations are ineffective for the reconstruction of meanings

When investigating a topic that cannot be quantitatively predicted, such as human nature, qualitative investigations are most effective (Gelo, Braakmann, & Benetka, 2008; Routledge, 2007).  Qualitative investigations are preferred for describing and interpreting experiences in context specific settings because each person's reality is construed in his or her own mind; qualitative research attempts to reveal the meanings that participants have given to various phenomena (Adams, 1999; Ponterotto, 2005).  This kind of information cannot be attained through quantitative analysis and requires the investigator to probe individuals for greater detail through in-depth interviews and open ended questions.

Theories are an organized body of principles and concepts intended to explain specific phenomena (Leedy & Ormrod, 2005).  Because theories help explain problems, they also provide possible solutions.  For example, if a researcher uses the social learning theory to describe crime, then the solution to the problem should be related to the social learning theory.  It makes no sense to claim that people learn to commit crime and then to suggest that providing people medicine (biological theory) is the solution.  In addition, the questions asked during a study should be related to the theoretical lens of the study.  If the questions asked on a survey, for example, are not related to the study, then the instrument may not be valid.

Null hypotheses are based on educated guesses and are used to assess research questions. However, because human knowledge is limited (i.e., there is an unknown number of extraneous variables), hypotheses cannot actually be proved true. Thus, researchers attempt to prove them false (Field, 2005; Shields, 2007). In other words, it can be shown that two variables are not related. However, if the two variables appear to be related, the relationship could be due to some other factors. In the courtroom, the jury can never be 100% sure that a person is guilty. Therefore, when the jury makes a guilty verdict, the jurors are saying that they have a certain confidence level that the defendant is not innocent.

Being not false is not the same thing as being true. In order words, if something is not negative, this does not mean that it is positive (i.e., it could be neutral). For example, if a sport team has played 10 games and is undefeated, what is the team's record? It is unknown because the team may have tied any number of the 10 games. If by some chance the team had tied all 10 games, a defense attorney may claim that the team has never lost, while the prosecutor may claim that the team has never won. Both statements are true, yet they seem contradictory. Indeed, the statements do not necessarily conflict with one another. This is how statistics can be misleading. Should consumers buy the same shoes used by the team? Either decision may be argued and supported with statistical data.

Results are not negative or positive if they are zero (neutral). Police officers need to detect diversionary flares (i.e., deception) that are intended to lead the officer off track. The way to do this is to get the sought-after answers. Questions and answers need to be presented in the active voice (American Psychological Association, 2010). For example, if an individual answers questions through double negatives or through misplaced modifiers, this may change the meaning of the statement. Notice in Table 1 that *"I have won"* $\neq$ *"I have not lost."*

Table 1. Interpretation of Sport Statement.

| | Interpretation of Results | | |
|---|---|---|---|
| | **Won (+)** | **Tied (neutral)** | **Lost (-)** |
| **Suspect statement** | | | |
| I have not lost | x | x | |
| I have not won | | x | x |
| I have won | x | | |
| I have lost | | | x |

Suppose I stated that the sky was not cloudy all day. All day means 100% of the time. Therefore, I am stating that it was not cloudy 100% of the time. It could have been cloudy 0% of the time up to 99% of the time. In other words, it could have been sunny 1% of the time up to 100% of the time. If you were investigating a case and it was important for the sky to be sunny, stating that the sky was not cloudy all day may be detrimental to your case. See Table 2 for an interpretation of the statement.

Table 2. Interpretation of Weather Statement.

| | Interpretation of Statement | | |
|---|---|---|---|
| | **Sunny all day** | **Cloudy up to 99% of time** | **Cloudy all day** |
| **Suspect statement** | | | |
| Not cloudy all day | x | x | |
| Not cloudy any part of day | x | | |

Now suppose that a police officer arrives at a crash scene. A car that was parked near a curb pulled out into traffic and was struck by another car headed in the same direction. Suppose the police officer asks a witness what she saw and she states, *"I did not see the driver in the parked car look before he pulled out into traffic."* The officer must evaluate the value of the statement. See Table 3 for an interpretation of the statement.

14

Table 3: Interpretation of Witness Statement.

| | Interpretation of Statement | |
| --- | --- | --- |
| | I was not looking | I was looking at driver and I saw driver not look |
| **Suspect statement** | | |
| I did not see the driver look | x | x |
| I saw the driver not look | | x |

Thus, the witness statement provided has little value. Notice the first four words: *"I did not see."* This is problematic because the police officer wants to know what the witness did see. Indeed, the witness statement never claimed that the driver of the parked car did not look before he pulled out into traffic. The witness statement would be true even if the witness was not looking in the right direction at the time of the crash. It would be wrong to assume that the witness was looking in the right direction. To argue in court that the witness saw the driver of the parked car not look would be changing the truth value of the witness statement. In short, a police officer needs to be careful about relying on assumptions. Hence, police officers need to get responses that provide direct and positive information.

**Verbs**

In police report writing, officers should use the active voice rather than the passive voice. This demonstrates clear and decisive actions taken by the police and may be perceived as confidence by jurors. A confident officer is perceived as a credible officer.

Preferred active voice: I arrested the suspect at the scene.
Non-preferred passive voice: The suspect was arrested at the scene by me.

**Being Clear About the Individuals Involved**

When writing a police report, it is especially important to be clear about each person involved. It is better to clarify individuals by name too often than to make the readers guess about who is being talked about. For example, consider the following information. Jon ran up to Tim and James, he struck him with his fist, and afterwards he cursed. It would seem that Jon struck either Tim or James, but the sentence does not make it clear. Furthermore, Jon, Tim, or James could have cursed. Thus, the information can be made much clearer if the individuals are identified by names. A better report would state that Jon ran up to Tim and James. With his fist, Jon then struck Tim. Afterwards, Tim cursed.

**Sound Natural**

Remember, the goal of a police report is to accurately document and communicate to the jurors the events that actually happened. This requires that police officers clearly communicate with the jurors. In addition, police officers must understand that jurors have emotions and these emotions may come into play in the courtroom. Therefore, a police officer must not alienate the jurors by writing in terms that are unclear or that create a gradient between the jurors and the officer. In short, jurors may not be familiar with law enforcement jargon and jurors may be negatively impacted by artificial or unnatural language. This may also apply to writing the police report in third person, which may appear to be unnatural. Although some police departments require reports to be written in third person for objectivity, other departments require reports to be written in first person, which may be more personal to the jurors. A police report written in third person is written for the police department while a police report written in first person is written for the jury. A report written in first person allows an officer to take ownership of the report.

Compare the following sentences.

Natural: I was notified by dispatch that there was a crash on US 20.

Unnatural: This unit was notified by dispatch that there was a 10-50 on US 20.

Natural: When I arrived at the scene, I parked my police car on the shoulder of the road.

Unnatural: When this unit went 10-23, this unit parked his commission on the berm.

Natural: I watched the home for an hour.

Unnatural: This unit engaged in visual surveillance of the residence for one hour.

16

Also, police officers must not assume that all individuals define words in the same way. For example, consider the following statements.

Clear: Where were you during supper?
Unclear: Where were you during dinner?

The latter sentence is problematic because dinner is not time dependent. Although supper is the last meal of the day, dinner is the largest meal of the day. Thus, for some people, dinner may not be the same as supper. In other words, if an officer asks a suspect several questions about his alibi during dinner time, the officer may be thinking about 5:00 pm and the suspect may be speaking about noon. Therefore, the police officer needs to make sure that the suspect correctly understands the questions that are being asked.

**Misplaced and dangling modifiers**

Grammar is important in police writing because an officer's credibility is linked to his or her written reports. As stated earlier, if police officers make mistakes in their reports, the officers should expect defense attorneys to ask them if they have performed their jobs to the best of their ability. On the one hand, if the officers claim that they have done their best work, then mistakes in their reports will make them appear incompetent or dishonest. On the other hand, if the officers claim that they have not done their best work, then mistakes in their reports will make them appear lazy and careless. Thus, police officers need to use proper grammar when writing police reports.

Because misplaced modifiers incorrectly modify the wrong words, and dangling modifiers have no referent in a sentence, misplaced and dangling modifiers may alter the meaning of a sentence (American Psychological Association, 2010). Thus, adjectives and adverbs should be placed as closely as possible to the words that they are supposed to modify and the active voice should be employed. This may help eliminate any unintended meanings.

Consider the following example.

*I told my wife that I loved her at the school.*

Intended meaning:  While at the school, I told my wife that I love her.

Perceived meaning: I told my wife that I love her being at the school.


The latter statement does not indicate that I love my wife but it does indicate that I love my wife's presence at school.  This would be appropriate, for example, if my wife worked at a school and I did not want her to quit her job and to leave the school.


Correct statement: I walked to the gas station because my car ran out of gas.

Incorrect statement: Running out of gas, I walked to the gas station.

The latter sentence indicates that I ran out of gas (not my car).  This may imply that I was jogging, I became tired, and I started to walk.


## Logic: Conditional Statements

The converse of a conditional statement is not necessarily true (Smith, Eggen, & St. Andre, 2006).  Although an if-then statement (if A, then B) may be true, the converse of the statement (if B, then A) may not necessarily be true.  For example, research shows that aggressive behaviors lead to arrest (Huesmann & Eron, 1992; Huesmann et al., 2002; Miller-Johnson et al., 2005).  Thus, if a person is aggressive, then the person will be arrested.  However, just because a person is arrested does not mean that the person was aggressive (e.g., there may be other reasons why the person was arrested).


## Examples: If the conditional statement is true, then is its converse true?


Conditional statement: If I am surfing, then I am in the water.
Converse statement: If I am in the water, then I am surfing.


Conditional statement: If I was sad, then I cried.
Converse statement: If I cried, then I was sad.

Conditional statement: If he is allowed to pass, then he has the document.

Converse statement: If he has the document, then he is allowed to pass.

Conditional statement: If you are the police, then you can arrest.

Converse statement: If you can arrest, then you are the police.

Conditional statement: If you are a professor, then you teach.

Converse statement: If you teach, then you are a professor.

Suppose I stated to my child that if she behaves then I will give her candy. Then suppose she misbehaves. Can I give her candy and still be truthful? Yes, I can give her candy and still be truthful. The only guarantee that I provided was that I will act in a certain way if she behaved. However, I never addressed what I will do if she misbehaved. Thus, if she misbehaves, my actions will be truthful whether or not I give her candy. I will only be untruthful if she did behave and I did not give her candy. This analogy becomes very important involving the passport law.

A non-American passport is issued by a foreign person's native country and is a travel document that is used for identification and proof of citizenship (LexisNexis, 2005). Federal law states that a passport is required for a nonimmigrant to enter the U.S. Thus, if a non-citizen has entered the U.S., then the non-citizen must have had a passport (this is a true statement). However, it is not necessarily true that if a non-citizen has a passport, then the non-citizen may automatically be allowed to enter the U.S. The law states that not having a passport will prevent a person from entering the U.S., but the law does not state that having a passport will allow a person to enter the U.S. See Table 4 for an interpretation of the law. Thus, understanding the converse of conditional statements is important in law enforcement.

Table 4. Interpretation of Law: *A nonimmigrant cannot enter the U.S. without a passport.*

| | Interpretation of Law | |
|---|---|---|
| | **If have, then will be allowed entry** | **If do not have, then will be denied entry** |
| Documents | | |
| Foreign Passport | Not Addressed | X |

## Quantifiers

An existential quantifier is not the same as a universal quantifier (Smith et al., 2006). It is important for police officers not to change the meaning of a statement by changing an existential quantifier statement into a universal quantifier statement. For an open sentence that uses an existential quantifier, the sentence is true if the truth set is nonempty, which means that the statement is true if the statement is true at least one time. However, for an open sentence that uses a universal quantifier, the sentence is true only if the truth set is the entire universe, which means that the statement is true only if the statement is true all of the time. For example, if a suspect stated that he likes beer, this statement is true if the suspect likes at least one type of beer. Thus, for the suspect to be lying, an officer will have to prove that the suspect dislikes all types of beer. However, if the suspect stated that he likes all beer, then the officer only needs to show that the suspect dislikes one type of beer for the suspect to be considered untruthful.

## Assumptions

All decisions depend on assumptions, and we will never know if the assumptions are 100% accurate. Although we may be confident about information, we cannot know with absolute certainty that the information is correct and complete. However, understanding the assumptions that were relied upon in making a decision is important because the assumptions may change, which may impact an objective decision. In law enforcement, if the assumptions change, then the police officers should be willing to modify their position.

Correlation does not mean causation (Leedy & Ormrod, 2005). Just because two events are highly correlated does not mean that one event causes the other. For example, it does not get dark at night because the sun is on the other side of the earth (Verma, 2005). The sun is an additional light source, but it is not the only light source in the sky. Thus, in this case, a wrong assumption may lead one to believe that the lack of sunlight causes it to get dark at night. Likewise, the amount of ice cream sold is positively related to the murder rate (Kentner, 2012). However, spending all of the department's resources to eliminate ice cream sales may not be very effective in addressing the murder rate.

## Error by design

Because human knowledge is limited, hypotheses cannot be proved true with 100% certainty (Field, 2005; Shields, 2007). However, given available information, statements can be proved false. If the hypotheses are not proved false, then they may be true (but we will never know with 100% certainty). In other words, if hypotheses are not proved false, then they are accepted as true at a certain confidence level.

Likewise, in court, we will never know with 100% certainty that a defendant is guilty of a crime (we will never know all of the variables that are involved). Indeed, evidence can be presented to show that the defendant is innocent (e.g., the defendant was already in prison at the time of the crime). However, if evidence is not presented to show that the defendant is innocent, and once a certain confidence level is reached that the defendant committed the crime (i.e., beyond a reasonable doubt), then the defendant may be convicted. This implies that there is an acceptable level of being wrong. Thus, innocent people will sometimes be wrongly convicted.

For a trial verdict, there are two possible ways to make a mistake. One way is to convict an innocent person. The other way is to set a guilty person free. A juror can only ensure that one type of error is never made, but this will require either a) always setting defendants free or b) always convicting defendants. For either case, there is no need for a trial. On the one hand, if one juror wants to ensure that he never makes a mistake by letting a guilty person go free, then that juror must always vote guilty. His reasoning may be that the police do not arrest innocent people. With this reasoning, there is no need for a trial because every person arrested will be convicted by this type of juror. On the other hand, if another juror wants to ensure that she never makes a mistake by sending an innocent person to jail, then that juror must always vote not guilty. With this reasoning, there is no need for a trial because every person arrested will be set free by this type of juror. Thus, in both cases, there is no need for a trial. However, there are trials in the U.S., which means that there is compromise and the chance of making mistakes.

Negotiations are required during jury deliberations. If a mistake is made, then the question is whether U.S. jurors want to error on the side of convicting innocent individuals or to error on the side of letting guilty individuals go free. By design, the U.S. legal system is set up to error on the side of letting guilty persons go free. A conviction is based on guilt beyond a reasonable doubt; an acquittal is not based on innocence beyond a reasonable doubt. As indicated in Figure 1, because decisions are based on confidence levels and negotiations, innocent individuals will sometimes be convicted. This is an inherent part of the U.S. legal system. Notice that this argument is not influenced by the penalty of the conviction, such as the death penalty. In other words, it is expected that innocent persons will sometimes be convicted and sentenced to death.

## Levels of Proof

Figure 1: Acceptable chance of wrongful conviction.

# CHAPTER 3. REPORT WRITING

The purpose of this book is to expose students to different types of police reports and forms. Instructors will need to help students work through the process of writing the narratives of various reports. The goal is for students to learn the process of report writing, which can be adapted to a particular department's needs. Also, by understanding what type of paperwork is required, students should anticipate the paperwork that will be required during various details. For example, students should expect to complete a property record and receipt form whenever evidence or property is collected.

Police report writing is not creative writing in the sense that all police reports have a consistent format. This format needs to be followed. Do not use creative writing to deviate from the standard format. Prosecutors collect reports from many different police departments, such as city police, county police, state police, conservation officers, and excise police. Thus, prosecutors need to be able to quickly and easily evaluate reports. In other words, information needs to be straightforward and presented in a consistent manner. Many different police forms within a department may contain the same information and consistency from form to form is quite important.

The state law book is a very valuable tool when enforcing state laws. The state law book provides the elements of a crime, which are needed when an officer completes affidavits and charging forms. The narrative should describe the particular crime, which must contain all of the required elements for that specific crime. For example, the elements of arson is not arson (never used a word to define itself). Likewise, arson is not setting fire to a building. If this were the case, firemen should be arrested during their training exercises. Therefore, the crime of arson must be looked up in the law book, which will provide the correct elements of the crime.

Police officers must report information accurately. Police officers must not change hearsay information into first-hand information. For example, if John told Mary that he was late for work because his car broke down, and if Mary told the supervisor that John was late because his car broke down, then Mary has changed the value of the information. Mary is testifying that John's car broke down. If John had lied to Mary and he was late because he had overslept, it is irrelevant as far as Mary's testimony is concerned. Mary should be held accountable for her statement. Mary stated that John's car broke down, which is a false statement. Mary should have stated that John told her that his car broke down, which is a true statement.

# Narratives of Select Reports

There is certain information that should be included in a police report, if the information is available. Officers should follow a consistent format. This will help ensure that all of the information is included in the report and it will also help make the report easier to read.

## Information on Crash Report

Because crash reports are available to the public, do not place criminal activity on a crash report. For example, DUI marijuana is a traffic violation but possession of marijuana is a criminal violation.

1) Date and time notified, location of crash investigation
2) Time arrived
3) What drivers stated (must include date, time, and location of crash)
4) What witnesses stated
5) What officer observed
6) What evidence indicated (do not place criminal activity on a crash report)
7) Description of damaged cargo and/or damaged property at scene (e.g., light pole)
8) Owner of damaged cargo and/or damaged property at scene (e.g., DOT)
9) What is the status of the vehicle? Who removed it from the scene?

If a report writer follows this format, it will not matter if a driver's statement does not match the evidence. The officer can still complete the report.

## Information on Crash Diagram

1) Location
2) North Always Faces Toward Top of Diagram (for consistency)  N↑
3) Not to scale
4) Point of impact
5) Solid lines before initial impact, dashed lines after initial impact
6) Measurements from a fixed reference point
7) Label all items on diagram

## Narrative of Case Report (criminal report)

1) Use the most serious charge to name the case
2) Describe Motive (e.g., personal gratification, revenge, greed, etc.) – why
3) Describe MO (strangled with cord, burned with gasoline, etc.) - how
4) List all additional suspects not already recorded on form
5) List all additional victims not already recorded on form
6) List all additional witnesses not already recorded on form
7) List all vehicles not already recorded on form

   *Begin Narrative*

8) Date and time notified, location of event
9) Time arrived
10) What victims stated (should talk to victim first to see if crime occurred)
11) What suspects stated
12) What witnesses stated
13) What officer observed
14) What the evidence indicates
15) What actions were taken by the officer
16) What evidence was collected
17) Where the evidence was stored
18) Status of vehicle (towed, removed by owner, etc.)
19) Copy of attachments (written statements, citations, charges, affidavits, etc.)

The case report is a criminal report and is not available to the public. The case report should mention that the suspect was double-locked handcuffed, the time the officer left the scene and arrived at the jail, and what the officer did with the evidence that was collected. This may reduce complaints against the officer and enhance the credibility of the report.

## Narrative of Incident Report (non-criminal report)

1) List all additional victims not already recorded on form
2) List all additional witnesses not already recorded on form
3) List all additional vehicles not already recorded on form

### *Begin Narrative*

4) Date and time notified, location of incident
5) Time arrived
6) What victims stated
7) What witnesses stated
8) What officer observed
9) What evidence indicates
10) What actions taken by officer
11) What evidence was collected
12) Where evidence was stored
13) Copy of attachments (written statements, property record and receipt form, etc.)

The incident report is a non-criminal report and is available to the public. An incident report should be completed when something non-criminal happens and should be documented. For example, lost or found property will require an incident report. The actual form may be the same as the case report form, but different information is recorded. Because it is a non-criminal report, there will be no motive, MO, or suspects.

## Intelligence Report (suspicious activity report)

1) Date and time notified, location of incident
2) Time arrived
3) What suspects stated
4) Associates of suspect
5) What officer observed
6) What evidence indicates
7) History of area (e.g., documented problem area)

The intelligence report is a suspicious activity report with reasonable suspicion that a crime has occurred or is likely to occur. There is no probable cause to make an arrest. The intelligence report is not available to the public. The purpose of the report is to gather and record information that may be used by police officers to solve crimes.

## Property Record & Receipt form

1) List items by number
2) Describe the sealed evidence from the outside and work inward
3) Start every line with, *One sealed plastic (paper) bag (box) containing...*
4) Describe evidence objectively (e.g., green plant material); let the experts in the lab identify the contraband

For example, if an officer uses a plastic bag to seal a plastic bag containing what a field test indicated was marijuana, then the officer will record the evidence as follows.

*Item 1: One sealed plastic bag containing a plastic bag containing green plant material.*

Lab personnel will testify as to what the lab results indicate. Remember, the property record and receipt is an official receipt of what the police officer has taken from the suspect. If the police officer indicates that he or she took marijuana and the drug is actually Khat, the suspect will show written proof in court that he never had Khat (the receipt indicates that it was marijuana). Indeed, the official police department receipt will prove the defendant's case. Also, if the officer takes a gold-colored watch, it is important that the officer not claim that the watch is gold just because it is gold in color.

## Lab Request

1) Describe items exactly as they were described on the Property Record & Receipt form

2) Tell the lab exactly what to do (use active language); do not make them guess

***Item 1: One sealed plastic bag containing a plastic bag containing green plant material.***

***Test item 1 for controlled substance.***
***Test item 2 for latent prints and DNA***

The lab receives many different pieces of evidence from many different departments that need to be tested. The police officer must not make the lab personnel guess about which tests to perform. If the tests are not specifically listed, do not expect that the tests will be performed. Every item to be tested should start in the same way: ***Test item # 1 for…***

## Firearm Report (e.g., for destruction of deer)

1) Date and time notified, location of incident

2) Time arrived

3) Witnesses (e.g., road maintenance, if at scene)

4) Indicate the type of animal injured

5) Traffic clear in all direction before firing gun (indicate safe distance)

6) Fired gun downward, away from traffic, and toward animal

7) Hit animal in proper location (as determined by department policy)

8) Number of shots fired

9) Animal destroyed

## Firearms Diagram

1) Indicate location
2) North always faces toward top of diagram (for consistency)
3) Not to scale
4) Draw area; include position of vehicles, individuals, and animal
5) Measurements from a fixed reference point
6) Label all items on diagram

## Probable Cause Affidavit and Charging Form

Some departments complete a) an application for an arrest warrant and b) an arrest warrant, while other departments complete a) a probable cause affidavit and b) a charging form. The process is basically the same. See Table 5. The difference between the two procedures is that in the former case, the arrest warrant is incorporated into the charging form and may be activated as soon as it is needed. In the latter case, the officer or prosecutor will complete an arrest warrant after the defendant has failed to comply with a court order or if the suspect cannot be found (e.g., if a suspect posted bail and failed to report to court, then an arrest warrant may be issued).

Table 5: Similarity between a Southern State and a Northern State.

| Southern State | | Northern State |
|---|---|---|
| Application for Arrest Warrant | = | Probable Cause Affidavit |
| Arrest Warrant | = | Charging Form (Information) <br> Arrest Warrant (only if needed) |

The elements of a crime, which are found in the state law book, must be described completely and accurately on the probable cause affidavit and charging forms. If the elements of the crime are not properly recorded on the probable cause affidavit and charging form, then the officer has failed to indicate a proper arrest. A police officer who arrests a person without properly charging the person may realize severe consequences.

In sum, police report writing is a process that can be adapted to any police department. Because police officers have different experiences, educational levels, and cultural experiences, probable cause may vary from officer to officer. Thus, officers must articulate their positions based on the available information, which includes a totality of circumstances. Police officers must engage in critical thinking, which is the open-minded, dynamic, and reflective process of collecting, analyzing, evaluating, and applying information in order to reach a reasonable decision. Critical thinking is used to establish probable cause and to make best-practice decisions.

# Plan of Action

Below is a plan of action for completing a DUI investigation that involves domestic violence. Of course, every case is unique and the events at the scene will be handled according to their seriousness and the chronological order in which they are presented. Police officers may divide and share the work load.

**At crash scene**

1) Conduct DUI investigation (issue citation for DUI, if probable cause found)

2) Complete crash report (will contribute to DUI probable cause affidavit)

3) Impound vehicle (impound form)

**At residence**

4) Photograph victim's injuries (create photo log)

5) Collect written statements from victims and witnesses, if possible

6) Collect evidence (property record & receipt form; photographs of property damage)

7) Case report (title of case will be most serious charge; at a minimum, domestic violence)

8) Notice of victim's rights (provided to victim at scene)

9) Victim's notification & waiver form (provided to victim at scene)

10) Suspected child abuse report (provided to family services)

11) Probable cause affidavit and charging form or 1) application for arrest warrant and 2) arrest warrant

12) DataMaster DUI Test (some departments arrest after the DataMaster test, some arrest before the test)

13) MUG Sheet/Photographs

14) Booking intake form (completed by jailer)

15) Custody Order / Custody Hold

16) Fingerprint card

17) Prisoner transfer form (completed a little later, if want to interrogate suspect)

### At court/post

18) Store evidence; complete lab request form (immediately after arrest)

19) Supplemental case report (completed a little later; updates; new information)

20) Final disposition form (reporting court decision; need court order to dispose of evidence)

# FORMAT OF NARRATIVES

**\*\*\*The narrative of every report should start with date, time, and location.\*\*\***

### Narrative of Firearms Report

On July 11, 2014 at about 3:00 am, I was notified by dispatch via radio that there was an injured deer on I-20 MP 11 in the north ditch. I arrived at the scene at about 3:33 am and I noticed a deer with mutilated legs near a fence in the north ditch. The deer was severely injured and suffering. Therefore, when traffic was clear in all direction for at least ½ mile, I used my department-owned Remington 12-gauge shotgun and fired one time, downward, toward the deer and away from traffic, hitting the deer in the head. The deer was destroyed and removed from the scene by highway maintenance.

## Narrative of Crash Report

On May 12, 2011 at about 2:00 am, I was notified by dispatch that there was a crash on I-20 MP 12 EB in Aiken County. I arrived at the scene at about 2:22 am and met with D1. D1 stated that on 5/12/2011 at about 1:50 am, he was eastbound on I-20 MP 12 when he came upon a deer standing on the roadway. D1 stated that he swerved to miss the deer and, as a result, he drove into the north ditch and hit the sign post. Also, D1 stated that he had a friend's $1,000 LuGusta vase in the vehicle that broke as a result of the crash.

Witness 1 stated that she was directly behind D1 at the time of the crash and that D1 was weaving for several miles prior to the crash. W1 stated that it appeared that D1 fell asleep because he gradually drove into the north ditch. W1 completed a written statement.

I observed the evidence at the scene and I noticed that the ruts in the sod along the highway indicated that D1 gradually drove into the north ditch. For over 200 yards, the ruts in the sod are only about 2 feet from the roadway's berm. Thus, the evidence indicates that D1 fell asleep and drove into the north ditch.

Involving the cargo, I observed that there was a red LuGusta vase in the vehicle that was damaged. D1 stated that the vase was owned by Jane Doe (provide personal information). Also, I observed that there was damage to 1) the state owned sod in the North Ditch at MP 12 and 2) the state owned sign post 24 at MP 12 EB (name, address, and phone number of the agency that owns the damaged property).

At 3:11 am, King Wench was called to remove the vehicle. King Wench arrived at 3:33 am and removed the vehicle from the scene.

## Narrative of Witness Statement - Example

On May 12, 2011 at about 2:00 am, I was on I-20 MP 12 heading EB in Aiken County. I was directly behind a red mustang and I observed the mustang weave for several miles, crossing over the skip lines from shoulder to shoulder. After several miles, the mustang gradually drove onto the grass in the north ditch and struck a sign post. I pulled over, called the police, and waited at the scene until the police arrived. There were no other individuals in the vehicle.

### Narrative of a Case Report: Example 1 = Possession of Marijuana with 1 Suspect

Prior to the narrative, state Motive and MO. Also, indicate additional suspects, witnesses, victims, and vehicles. **Note: The state is the victim for drug cases.**

**Motive:** personal satisfaction

**MO**: suspect transported marijuana in vehicle

**Witnesses**: none

On August 2, 2013 at about 1:11 am, I used radar and I clocked a blue Chevy Caprice on I-20 MP 5 WB in Aiken County at 99 MPH in a 70 MPH zone. I initiated my police car's emergency lights and stopped the vehicle at MP 2 WB. I approached the driver of the vehicle and I immediately noticed what appeared to be a bag of marijuana in front ash tray. I asked the driver for his driver's license and he handed me his MI driver's license, which identified the driver as John DOE (DOB = 1/5/1971). I asked DOE, and sole occupant of the vehicle, what he had in the bag in the front ash tray. DOE stated that it was marijuana and he handed me the bag. From my experience as a police officer, the green leafy substance did look and smell like marijuana. I asked DOE to exit the vehicle, and he complied. I double-locked handcuffed DOE and secured him in my police vehicle. I secured the evidence as indicated on PRR 11073. I left the scene at about 1:30 am and I transported DOE to the Aiken County jail. I arrived at the jail at about 1:44 am.

At about 2:44 am, after the booking process, I immediately transported the evidence to the Aiken City Police post, as indicated on property record and receipt 11073 . I returned to I-20 MP 2 WB at about 3:00 am. Dispatch contacted King Wench, who removed the vehicle from the scene at about 3:30 am, as indicated on impound form 4838.

### Narrative of Case Report:  Example 2 – Possession of Marijuana with 2 Suspects

*When checking the Aiken Café's parking lot, you notice two suspects sitting in a car in the parking lot smoking what appears to be marijuana. You arrest both the suspects for possession of controlled substance.*

**Motive** (Why did this crime happen?):  Self gratification

**M.O.** (How did this crime happen?): Smoking marijuana in parked vehicle

On 7-11-2013 at about 11:01 am, I was patrolling the parking lot of Aiken café, which is located at 122 Laurens Street in Aiken, SC.  I came upon a black 2 door Ford Mustang that was occupied by two females who appeared to be smoking marijuana.  I exited my police car and approached the occupants.  When the driver rolled down her widow, I could immediately smell the odor of burnt marijuana.  I asked both occupants for their identifications and both occupants provide me their SC driver's licenses.  The driver was identified as Jane DOE (w/f/DOB = 3/3/1977; SC DL 47347) and the passenger was identified as Jonnie JONES (h/f/DOB 4/4/1981; SC DL 58480).  I asked DOE if she had any marijuana in the vehicle and she stated that she did.  DOE opened the center console and handed me a bag of green plant material.  From my training and experience as a law enforcer, the bag of green plant material did look and smell like marijuana.  I asked DOE if the bag of green plant material was hers, and she stated that it was hers.

I then asked JONES, who was sitting in the front passenger seat, if she had any marijuana. JONES stated that she did.  JONES reached under the front passenger seat and then handed me a bag of green plant material.  From my training and experience as a law enforcer, the bag of green plant material from JONES did look and smell like marijuana.  At that time, I double-locked handcuffed both occupants, and I secured them in the back of my police car.  I then performed a NIK Marijuana Field Test on each bag of green plant material, which indicated positive for marijuana.  At about 11:22 am, I arrested both occupants for possession of controlled substance.  I secured the evidence from DOE as indicated on PRR 2192.   I secured the evidence from JONES as indicated on PRR 362.   At about 11:25 am, Trooper

Sheila Smith (434) arrived at the scene and she searched both suspects. After the search, at about 11:31 am, I transported both suspects to the Aiken County jail. I arrived at the jail at about 11:42 am.

At about 12:39 pm I arrived back at 122 Laurens Street in Aiken, SC and I called King Wench to tow the suspect's vehicle. King Wench arrived at the scene at about 1:11 pm and removed the vehicle at about 1:28 pm. The address of King Wench is 132 Wrecker Lane Aiken, SC 29801 (803-555-6753).

At about 1:30 pm, I transported the evidence to Aiken City Police Department. I secured the evidence for PRR 2192 in locker 1. I secured the evidence for PRR 362 in locker 4.

## Questions that a supervisor may ask the officer after reading the report:

1) Is the report written in chronological order? Start with date, time, and location.

2) How did you know it was contraband? Training, experience, and field test.

3) Where are the drugs? Did you secure them at the post or lab?

4) Where is the car? Was it towed or did you leave it for the driver to remove?

5) Did you double-lock handcuff the suspects? There is an injury complaint.

6) Did you search/frisk the suspects? If a suspect is touched, it should be documented.

7) Does department policy allow an officer to search the opposite sex? Call same sex officer.

8) How long did it take for you to transport the suspects to jail? There is a sexual complaint.

# CHAPTER 4. POLICE REPORTS

**Layout of Reports**

# ADMINISTRATIVE REPORTS

# Police Department Assignment Card* (example)
## February 14, 2014

| Event | Time |
|-------|------|
| Patron reported crash I-80 MP 144 EB | 0800 |
| 11-43 notified – en route from MP 111 | 0802 |
| 11-43 arrived at scene | 0822 |
| Wrecker called (Tom's) | 0843 |
| Wrecker arrived at scene | 0921 |
| Wrecker left scene w/driver | 0944 |
| 11-43 cleared scene | 0948 |

*This provides a record of events with associated times.

---

## Assignment Card

Complete an assignment card for a crash at I-20 MP 11 in the south ditch. There were injuries, an ambulance was called, the Fire Department was called, a HazMat scene was declared, a state DNR representative was contacted, state DOT were contacted, a HazMat cleanup crew was contacted, and a wrecker for the vehicle was contacted.

# Police Daily Activity Report

Month _____ Year _____ Shift    M    D    A    Special Patrol

Officer: _____ Badge _____ District _____

## Activity

| | | | |
|---|---|---|---|
| Total Citations | | Crashes Investigated | |
| Moving Citations | | Crash Citations | |
| Total Seatbelt Citations | | Total Criminal Arrests | |
| Child Restraint Citations | | Felony Arrests | |
| Driver's License Citations | | Drug Arrests | |
| Driving While Suspended Citations | | DUI arrests | |
| Commercial Motor Vehicle Citations | | Alco-sensor Tests | |
| Total Warnings | | DataMaster Tests | |
| Moving Warnings | | Number of Case Reports | |
| Total Seatbelt Warnings | | Number of Details | |
| Child Restraint Warnings | | Number of Medical Calls | |
| Commercial Motor Vehicle Warnings | | Number of Intelligence Reports | |
| Police Services | | Number of Traffic Dispositions | |
| Public Information Presentations | | Number of Stolen Vehicles Recovered | |

## Hours

| Total Patrol Hrs. | | Crash Report Hrs. | | Case Report Hrs. | | Criminal Investigation Hrs. | | Incident Investigation Hrs. | | Court Hrs. | |
|---|---|---|---|---|---|---|---|---|---|---|---|
| Mileage Start | | Mileage End | | Special Project Mileage Start | | Special Project Mileage End | | Total Mileage for day | | Meal Hrs. | |

# Police Employee Personal Illness or Injury

| Officer's Name (Last/First/MI) | Badge # | Rank | County |
|---|---|---|---|
| Date of Illness/Injury | Time of Illness/Injury | Date Failed to Report to Work | Time of Day Failed to Report to Work |

| Total Number of Hours Failed to Report to Work | Status (Check all that apply) | Type of Report |
|---|---|---|
| | ◊ Illness  ◊ Injury  ◊ Family  <br><br> ◊ Line-of-duty  ◊ Non-line-of-duty | ◊ Original <br><br> ◊ Supplemental |
| Examined by Physician? <br><br> ◊ No <br><br> ◊ Yes | Name of Physician <br><br><br> Location of Treatment | Place of Confinement (Home, Hospital Name, etc.) |

**Give complete details pertaining to illness or injury.**

| Officer Submitting Report | Badge | Date of Report | Employee Signature |
|---|---|---|---|
| | | | |

40

# Police Vehicle and Equipment Form

| Date | Time | Beginning Mileage | |
|---|---|---|---|
| Shift:  M   D   A   SP | Car | Driver | |
| Cones        Y       N | Vests     Y       N | Shotgun    Y       N | Spare Tire    Y       N |
| Fire Extinguisher   Y    N | Camera    Y       N | First Aid Kit    Y       N | Evidence Kit   Y    N |
| Light Bars    Y     N | Car Lights   Y    N | Flashlight      Y   N    /   Siren     Y   N | Radar      Y       N |
| CPR Breath Mask   Y    N | AED    Y       N | Body Damage to Car       Y       N  (if damage, describe): | |

Unit Check for Contraband       Y       N

Comments

| Officer | Badge | Officer's Signature |
|---|---|---|

# Affidavit of Citizen Complaint

_____Police Department

I swear under penalty of law that the following statement is true.

_____

_____

_____

_____

_____

_____

_____

_____

_____

_____

I,_____ (name), DOB: _____ ID: _____

(check only one below)

____as indicated by my signature below

or

_____ as informed by police and recorded on police telephone line (if check this box, read
information below over recorded telephone line)

state that this affidavit for complaint is true, and I request an investigation of the matters
contained within. I understand this affidavit is an official police report and may be subject to
public disclosure upon request. I am advised that if the allegations contained within are
proven to be untrue, and if this affidavit contains deliberate falsehoods or is made with
malicious intent, I may be subject to criminal charges and/or civil liability.

Signed (Print Name of Complainant if called in):_____ Date: _____

Witness: _____ Date: _____

# COMMENDATION/COMPLAINT FORM

## _____POLICE DEPARTMENT

***ALL COMPLAINTS MAY BE SUBJECT TO PUBLIC DISCLOSURE***

NATURE OF REPORT: __ COMMENDATION __ COMPLAINT

SUPERVISOR TAKING REPORT:_____

__ IN PERSON __ TELEPHONE __ LETTER ___ ANONYMOUS

INCIDENT

LOCATION:_____

INCIDENT DATE:_____ INCIDENT TIME:_____

CASE#_____

NAME OF PERSON MAKING

REPORT:_____

PHONE (H)_____ (W)_____

ADDRESS:_____

| OFFICERS INVOLVED | | |
|---|---|---|
| NAME | BADGE # | RANK |
| | | |
| | | |
| | | |
| | | |
| WITNESSES | | |
| NAME | ADDRESS | PHONE # |
| | | |
| | | |
| | | |
| | | |

DESCRIPTION OF ALLEGED INCIDENT:_____

_____

_____

_____

_____

_____

_____

_____

_____

_____

_____

_____

ATTACHMENTS:

___ NONE

___ STATEMENTS

___ EVIDENCE

___OTHER_____

_____     _____     _____
Signature of Officer Completing this Report     Badge #          Date

44

# SUPERVISOR INVESTIGATION REPORT

**INSTRUCTIONS:** TO BE COMPLETED BY THE SUPERVISOR INVESTIGATING AN ALLEGATION OF RULES VIOLATIONS BY ONE OF HIS/HER EMPLOYEES.

**TYPE OF COMPLAINT** (CHECK ALL THAT APPLY)

\_\_ ABUSE OF AUTHORITY  \_\_ALCOHOL/DRUG USE  \_\_ BIASED-BASED POLICING

\_\_CONDUCT TOWARDS OTHERS  \_\_\_CRIMINAL ACTIVITY \_\_ GRATUITIES \_\_\_ HONESTY

\_\_ INSUBORDINATION \_\_ NEGLECT OF DUTY \_\_ OFF-DUTY CONDUCT-GENERAL

\_\_ UNBECOMING CONDUCT \_\_\_ USE OF FORCE/EXCESSIVE \_\_OTHER_____


INVESTIGATING SUPERVISOR:_____ RANK:_____

DATE COMPLAINT WAS RECEIVED:_____ TIME RECEIVED:_____

_____

**FINDINGS**:_____

## RECOMMENDATION AS TO CONCLUSION OF FACT

___ SUSTAINED................... EVIDENCE SUFFICIENT TO PROVE THE ALLEGATION

___ NOT SUSTAINED............ INSUFFICIENT EVIDENCE TO EITHER PROVE OR DISPROVE

___ EXONERATED............... INCIDENT OCCURRED, BUT WAS LAWFUL.

___ UNFOUNDED................ ALLEGATION IS FALSE

ATTACHMENTS:

___ NONE

___ STATEMENTS

___ EVIDENCE

___ OTHER_____

SUPERVISOR'S SIGNATURE: _____ DATE: _____

# EMPLOYEE DISCIPLINARY REPORT

The following was issued today and it is to be made part of the official record.    ☐Warning    ☐Separation

_____

NAME                    BADGE                    DEPARTMENT                         DATE


1. ___ Unreported Absence          2. ___ Tardiness                3. ___ Drinking on Duty

4. ___ Dishonesty                  5. ___ Improper Conduct         6. ___ Carelessness

7. ___ Violation of Safety Rules   8. ___ Leaving Without Permission   9. ___ Unbecoming of an officer

10. ___ Insubordination            11. ___ Failure to Obey Orders   12. ___ Defective and Improper Work

13. ___ Reporting Under the Influence of Alcohol    14. ___ Other (Describe) _____


REMARKS    (Describe Details)

_____
_____
_____
_____
_____
_____
_____
_____
_____
_____
_____
_____
_____
_____
_____


I have read this report:     _____    _____
                              Signature of Supervisor          Signature of Employee

# FIELD TRAINING OFFICER (FTO) DAILY OBSERVATIONS

## _____POLICE DEPARTMENT TRAINEE EVALUATION

TRAINEE'S NAME          BADGE        FTO'S NAME         BADGE

DATE _____        SHIFT: ☐ DAY   ☐ AFTERNOON   ☐ MIDNIGHT

| NOT ACCEPTABLE | ACCEPTABLE | SUPERIOR |
|---|---|---|
| 1 | 2 | 3 |

## GENERAL
Rating ___ 1. GENERAL APPEARANCE

## ATTITUDE
Rating ___ 2. ACCEPTANCE OF FEEDBACK FTO/FTO PROGRAM
Rating ___ 3. ATTITUDE TOWARD POLICE WORK

## KNOWLEDGE
Rating ___ 4. KNOWLEDGE OF DEPARTMENT POLICIES AND PROCEDURES
Rating ___ 5. KNOWLEDGE OF CRIMINAL STATUES
Rating ___ 6. KNOWLEDGE OF TRAFFIC CODES
Rating ___ 7. KNOWLEDGE OF CODES OF CRIMINAL PROCEDURE

## PERFORMANCE
Rating ___ 8. DRIVING SKILLS: NORMAL CONDITIONS
Rating ___ 9. DRIVING SKILLS: MODERATE/HIGH STRESS
Rating ___ 10. RESPONSE TIME TO CALLS
Rating ___ 11. ROUTINE FORMS: ACCURACY / COMPLETENESS
Rating ___ 12. REPORT WRITING: ORGANIZATION / DETAILS
Rating ___ 13. REPORT WRITING: GRAMMAR / SPELLING/ NEATNESS
Rating ___ 14. REPORT WRITING: APPROPRIATE TIME USED
Rating ___ 15. FIELD PERFORMANCE: NON-STRESS CONDITIONS
Rating ___ 16. FIELD PERFORMANCE: STRESS CONDITIONS
Rating ___ 17. INTERVIEW SKILLS
Rating ___ 18. INTERVIEW/INTERROGATION SKILL
Rating ___ 19. SELF-INITIATED FIELD ACTIVITY
Rating ___ 20. OFFICER SAFETY: GENERAL
Rating ___ 21. OFFICER SAFETY: SUSPECTS/SUSPICIOUS PERSONS/PRISONERS
Rating ___ 22. CONTROL ON CONFLICT: VOICE COMMAND
Rating ___ 23. CONTROL ON CONFLICT: PHYSICAL SKILL
Rating ___ 24. PROBLEM SOLVING / DECISION MAKING
Rating ___ 25. RADIO: APPROPRIATE USE OF CODES / PROCEDURE
Rating ___ 26. RADIO: LISTENS AND COMPREHENDS

## RELATIONSHIPS
Rating ___ 27. WITH CITIZENS IN GENERAL
Rating ___ 28. WITH ETHNIC/ CULTURAL / SOCIAL GROUPS
Rating ___ 29. WITH OTHER DEPARTMENT MEMBERS

Daily Average Rating _____

FTO'S NOTES:


TRAINEE'S SIGNATURE      BADGE      FTO'S SIGNATURE      BADGE

# PUBLIC SERVICE REPORTS

# Public Speaker - Community Relations Form

| Sponsoring Organization | Date | Time |
|---|---|---|
| Speaker's Name | | Badge |
| Badge Numbers of Assisting Officers | | |
| Location of Event | | County |
| Program Date | | Program Length of Time |
| Program Title | | |
| Activities | | |
| Name of Handout Material | | |
| Audience (Name of Group) | | |
| Number in Attendance | | Age Range of Group |
| Audience or Community Comments | | |

Topic of Presentation (circle one)

|  |  |  |
|---|---|---|
| Traffic Safety | Crime Prevention | Youth Services |
| Substance Abuse | Recruiting | Community Education |

Traffic Safety (e.g., Seatbelt use)

Crime Prevention (e.g., Lock your doors)

Youth services (e.g., Midnight basketball program)

Substance Abuse (e.g., Say "no" to drugs)

Recruiting (e.g., Academy standards and demand for particular skills)

Community Education (e.g., New trash recycling laws)

# Police Service Report
## _____Police Department

☐On Duty          Date _____

☐Off Duty         Time _____

Vehicle _____
      (Color)     (Year)     (Make)

License Plate _____ _____ State _____

Name _____

Address _____

Location _____
      (Highway)        County

Service Needed/Problem _____
            (Out of gas, flat tire, etc.)

_____

Action Provided _____

_____

Officer _____ Badge _____

# Police Courtesy Notification

_____ Police Department

The vehicle described below has been observed parked in the parking lot
 in the following condition:


_____the vehicle is unlocked.

_____personal items of apparent value are visible through the windows.

_____vehicle appears to have been abandoned.

_____ (other):_____


Vehicle: _____
          Color       Make      Model      Year

_____
        License               State

The above condition is an invitation to theft and/or vandalism.
Please safeguard your vehicle and property by keeping your vehicle
locked, by placing personal items out of sight,  and by parking in a
spot visible from the building.



Officer & Badge : ___  _____

# ABANDONED VEHICLE NOTICE

| | |
|---|---|
| _____ Police Department | |
| ABANDONED VEHICLE NOTICE | |
| STATE & LICENSE | |
| DATE | |
| TIME | |
| OFFICER | |
| DEPARTMENT ADDRESS | |
| DEPARTMENT PHONE | |

IF THIS ABANDONED VEHICLE IS NOT REMOVED WITHIN

□ 2    □ 24    □ 48    □ 72    □ Other ____    **HOURS**

FROM THE TIME THIS NOTICE IS POSTED, IT WILL BE

IMPOUNDED.

# BREAK-UP PERMIT

## DEPARTMENT OF TRANSPORTATION

### TRACTOR-TRAILER BREAK-UP PARKING PERMIT
### (USED ON TURNPIKE TO ACCOUNT FOR # AXLES ENTERING & LEAVING)

COMPANY NAME

ADDRESS

CITY                                                                    STATE

MOTORIZED UNIT LICENSE #     # OF AXLES     TRAILER LICENSE #     # OF AXLES

DRIVER'S SIGNATURE

## IS SATISFACTORILY PARKED ☐ YES   ☐ NO  DATE_____

ROADWAY _____

NEAR MILEPOST NO._____     ____EB    ____WB    ____NB    ____SB

AT SERVICE AREA _____

POLICE OFFICER SIGNATURE                                    BADGE #

## Exiting Turnpike

LANE NO.                          DATE                          TIME

ATTENDANT'S SIGNATURE                                       BADGE #

TIME LIMIT FOR THIS PERMIT _____ HOURS.

OFFICER_____ BADGE # _____

## TIME LIMIT SHALL NOT EXCEED 72 HOURS

# POLICE OFFICER AFFIDAVIT for TITLE

**Physical Inspection of Resident's** ☐ **Vehicle** ☐ **Watercraft** **in order to Obtain Title**

The purpose of this form is to confirm information about the applicant and the vehicle or watercraft so that a title for the vehicle or watercraft may be obtained. Used for vehicles or watercraft with no title or lost titles. After the form is complete, the police officer will submit it to the BMV/DMV/Secretary of State.

**Person Requesting Title**

Name of Person requesting a title for vehicle ownership: _____

Address: _____

DOB _____ SSN _____

Driver's License _____ _____ State _____

**Vehicle Information**

Vehicle: Year _____ Make _____ Model _____

Type (RV, motorcycle, etc.) _____

Last registration on vehicle _____ State _____

☐ VIN ☐ HIN (HULL) _____

**Vehicle Check**

☐ VIN ☐ HIN Checked on Computer for Cleared Status _____ Yes ___ No

☐ Vehicle ☐ Watercraft Cleared to Title ___ Yes ___ No

*To: BMV/DMV/Secretary of State. I affirm that the above information is true.*

Printed name of inspecting police officer _____

Police Officer's Signature _____ Date _____

Department _____ Badge _____ ___

# LAW ENFORCEMENT DEMAND FOR DRIVER RE-EXAMINATION

A Police Officer's request for Re-Examination is allowed based on the officer's observation of a driver who may have a mental or physical problem that affects his/her driving ability.

TO: DMV/BMV/Secretary of State

FROM:_____
Police Officer (Name & Badge #)                                      Rank

_____
POLICE DEPT                ADDRESS                           PHONE #

Driver _____
Name                       Address

Race_____ Sex_____ DOB_____ DL#_____

On_____ _____ At_____ ___.M.
(Month)          (Date)              (Year)

Based on my observation(s) of the above named driver I have concerns that the driver may have a mental or physical problem that affects his/her ability to safely operate a motor vehicle.

Was this the result of a traffic accident?      □ YES      □ NO
Was this the result of a traffic violation?     □ YES      □ NO
Was a summons issued?                           □ YES      □ NO

_____
Police Officer Signature       Badge #              Department

## TO BE COMPLETED BY THE DEPARTMENT OF MOTOR VEHICLE

RESULT OF DEMAND:   □ YES, DRIVER REQUIRED TO ATTEND      □ NO, DRIVER NOT REQUIRED TO ATTEND

_____     _____
Name of Dept. of Motor Vehicle Supervisor     Dept. of Motor Vehicle Supervisor Signature

_____     _____
Date                                          Agency

# Salvation Army Voucher

*Travelers' Assistance Program*

| Police Department | Date | Time |
|---|---|---|
| Salvation Army Authorization | Describe Need | |
| Name & Location that Provided Service | County where services were rendered | |
| Maximum Amount Granted $ | Services Provided and Amount for Each Service Provided | |

| **Name of Individual Receiving Assistance** | | | |
|---|---|---|---|
| Address | | Phone | |
| Driver's License | State | SSN | |
| DOB | SEX | | Race |
| Vehicle Make | Model | VIN | |
| Color | License Plate | State of Plate | |
| Owner of Vehicle | | Owner at Scene    Y        N | |
| **Merchant Name** | | | |
| Merchant Address (HQ) | | | |

Driver's Signature _____

Officer's Signature _____ Badge _____ Date _____

Merchant: For payment, send itemized voucher to Salvation Army (only authorized services will be reimbursed).

# Permit for Possession of Deer

_____Department

| Recipient's Name | Date |
|---|---|
| Recipient's Address | Date of Birth |
| Vehicle Make & Model | Driver's License State & Number |
| Vehicle Year | License Plate State & Number |
| Sex of Deer<br><br>☐Male    ☐Female | ☐Highway Kill<br><br>☐ Illegal Kill<br><br>☐ Destroyed by Police<br><br>☐Other _____ |
| Recipient's Signature | |
| Signature of Officer Issuing Permit & Badge | Agency of Officer |

Any deer with antlers less than 1" in length is considered a doe.

# Courtesy Summons

_____ Police Department

Cause _____ _____

To: _____ DOB: _____

Address: _____

City: _____ State: _____ Zip: _____

Date: _____ Time: _____ Location Served: _____

SSN: _____ DL: _____ _____ DL State: _____

Phone: _____ Sex: _____ Race: _____

**State of** _____ **◊ County of** _____ **◊ City of** _____


**YOU ARE HEREBY COMMANDED** to be and appear in your person before the

Honorable _____, _____ Court Judge, at

(address) _____ on the _____ day

of _____, 20_____ at _____ o'clock A.M. in response to

_____ vs. _____ involving the

offense(s) of (title of offense) _____

being in violation of statute/code _____.


I understand that I am charged with a violation of a ☐ state law ☐ local ordinance ☐ both.

This summons is being issued as a courtesy. Failure to appear will be followed by an arrest warrant

being served.


_____
Printed Name of Defendant

_____                    _____
Printed Name of Officer                                         Badge


_____
Signature of Defendant

_____
Signature of Officer

# TRAFFIC INVESTIGATION REPORTS

# POLICE COMPLAINT - INFORMATION SUMMONS

| Court | Cause # (to be issued by court) |
|---|---|

☐ Complaint (Traffic)    ☐ Information (Criminal)    County of _____    City of _____

*I have probable cause to believe that on*

| Weekday | Day of Month | Month | Year | Time |
|---|---|---|---|---|
| Last Name | | First Name | | MI |

| Home Street Address | | | | |
|---|---|---|---|---|
| City | | State | | Zip Code |
| Race | Sex | Height | Weight | DOB | | Age |

| ☐ DL  ☐ State ID  ☐ SSN  ☐ Other _____  Number: _____ | State | ☐ Commercial DL    ☐ Operator's DL | CDL Class |
|---|---|---|---|

☐ Did unlawfully operate    ☐ Committed a violation as a passenger    in a vehicle described as

| Color | Vehicle Year | Make | License expiration year | License state | License plate # |
|---|---|---|---|---|---|

| ☐ Passenger Car/Pickup truck | ☐ Tractor   ☐ Tractor-trailer   ☐ Straight truck   ☐ Bus   ☐ Other |
|---|---|
| | ☐ DOT #   ☐ ICC # _____   ☐ Hazmat Placard # |

At Location

## DID COMMIT THE FOLLOWING VIOLATION

| Vehicle Speed | Speed Limit |
|---|---|

Description of Offense:

In Violation of Statute/Code:

*I affirm under penalty of perjury that the above information is true*

| Signature of Officer | Print Name | Police Dept. | Badge # |
|---|---|---|---|
| Court | Court Address & Phone # | Respond to Court By (date) | |

| Violator's Signature COURT APPEARANCE PROMISE | *I promise to appear before the court when required. My signature is not an admission of guilt.* | **Approved by Solicitor/Prosecutor** Signature: _____  Date: _____ |
|---|---|---|

# TRAFFIC VIOLATIONS – COURT NOTICE

## (Attach to Traffic Citation)

_____ Court

Address _____

Phone _____

1. You must return the citation with your payment to the above address within 30 days of the date of issue.

2. You must request a trial date if you want to contest the citation.

3. If you want to admit the charge, mail the citation with payment. If you want to contest the charge, sign the back of the citation, request a court date, and mail the citation without payment.

4. Failure to respond will result in increased penalties.

5. Schedule of Costs

   **Speed**

   1-5 MPH over ................. $200

   6-10 MPH over .............. $300

   11-24 MPH over ............. $500

   25+ MPH over .............. Mandatory court appearance

   Parking ....................... $150

   Handicapped Parking ........ $500

   Passing Violation ............. $300

   Unsafe lane movement....... $300

   Other Violations ............. Call Court

# POLICE TRAFFIC WARNING

County of _____ City of _____

*I have probable cause to believe that on*

| Weekday | Day of Month | Month | Year | Time |
|---|---|---|---|---|
| Last Name | | First Name | | MI |

| Home Street Address |
|---|

| City | | State | Zip Code |
|---|---|---|---|

| Race | Sex | Height | Weight | DOB | Age |
|---|---|---|---|---|---|

| ☐ DL  ☐ State ID  ☐ SSN  ☐ Other _____  Number: _____ | State | ☐ Operator's DL  ☐ Commercial DL | CDL Class |
|---|---|---|---|

☐ Did unlawfully operate   ☐ Committed a violation as a passenger     in a vehicle described as

| Color | Vehicle Year | Make | License expiration year | License state | License plate # |
|---|---|---|---|---|---|

☐ Passenger Car/Pickup truck   ☐ Tractor   ☐ Tractor-trailer   ☐ Straight truck   ☐ Bus   ☐ other____

At Location

| **Moving Violation** | **Non-Moving Violation** | **Equipment Violation** |
|---|---|---|
| ☐ Speed | ☐ Seatbelt | ☐ Headlights |
| ☐ Following Too Close | ☐ Parking | ☐ Tail Lights |
| ☐ Lane Movement | ☐ Driver's License | ☐ Brake Lights |
| ☐ Traffic Control Device | ☐ Registration | ☐ Muffler |
| ☐ Passing | ☐ Insurance | ☐ Windshield |
| ☐ Other _____ | ☐ Other _____ | ☐ Other |

| Details of Violation(s) | Code (primary) |
|---|---|

| Officer's Signature | Print Name | Police Agency | Badge # |
|---|---|---|---|

*Correct all violations immediately!*

63

# Crash Definitions/Rules for Reference

Crash number will be issued by the post or by the computer during electronic submission

**5 items required on crash diagram** = 1) Location (top-center), 2) NTS (not to scale), 3) N↑ (always faces upward), 4) measurements (at least two), 5) POI (point of initial impact)

Draw vehicles from top view (if can see the vehicle's wheels, then the vehicle is not upright)

Make north point upward on the crash diagram. This will make all crash reports consistent and easier for others to read.

Crash report required if total damage ≥ $1,000 or if someone requests it (damage required)

When the actions stops, the crash is over

Trailer = being pulled (not using a motor at time of crash) + touching ground

Vehicle 1 = at fault, if there is a vehicle at fault

Cargo = being hauled + not touching the ground

Solid line = prior to crash; Dashed line = after initial impact

Draw the vehicles before crash, at initial impact, and at final rest (if practical)

If vehicle left scene (e.g., car-deer crash), look for evidence (e.g., deer hair on car). Actual location of crash may be unknown and may be impossible to find – only measurements available may be roadway. Only need to draw vehicle and deer prior to crash and at initial impact (based on driver's statement). At a minimum, draw vehicle prior to POI and at POI; it may not be necessary to draw a vehicle at final rest if vehicle did not stop and left scene (e.g., car versus deer crash).

Measure all important distances, marks, debris, and other items at a crash scene from fixed reference points (points that will not likely move). Do not use the vehicle as the reference point (even if it is parked because it can easily be moved). At a minimum, there should be at least 2 measurements on diagram (e.g., width of road and berms for car-deer crash when the car has left the crash scene).

Draw a sketch of the scene and use straight lines at the scene to take the measurements as easily and quickly as possible; the scene can be rotated on the final drawing to face north at a later time.

Label all items/group of items on diagram (e.g., may label one parking line to represent group). Be clear.

Arrow inside vehicle indicates directions vehicle is facing

**Initial Impact + Vehicle Damage** boxes will be completed for each vehicle involved

Other participant = someone who influenced the crash but who was not part of the actual crash. For example, ice comes off of a tractor-trailer and hits a car. The tractor-trailer did not make contact with anything and is not directly involved with the crash. Information about the tractor-trailer and its driver will be included in the report as other participant. This scenario will be a one vehicle collision crash.

Record what drivers/witnesses say – do not change what they say to meet your agenda

Collision crash = vehicle impacted something that caused damage; Non-collision crash = vehicle did not impact something that caused damage. Vehicle cannot collide with roadway surface or ground surface (however, a vehicle can collide with an earth embankment, dirt pile, etc.). Vehicle cannot collide with itself (e.g., jackknife).

No crash report for flat tires; however, crash report may be required for damaged rims

May write report in either 1st or 3rd person. First person is better for the jury (more personalized); third person is better for the police department (seems more objective)


## Information on Crash Report

Date and time notified, location of crash investigation

Time arrived

What drivers stated (must include date, time, and location of crash)

What witnesses stated

What officer observed

What evidence indicated (do not place criminal activity on a crash report)

Description of damaged cargo and/or damaged property at scene (e.g., light pole)

Owner of damaged cargo and/or damaged property at scene (e.g., DOT)

Status of vehicles (state if impounded or removed from scene by drivers)


If the report writer follows this format, it will not matter if the driver's statement does not match the evidence. The officer can still complete the report.

**Information on Crash Diagram**

Location

North Always Faces Toward Top of Diagram (for consistency)  N↑

Not to scale

Point of initial impact

Measurements from a fixed reference point (indicate a minimum of at least two measurements)

Solid lines before initial impact, dashed lines after initial impact

Label all items on diagram

# Information Required on Crash Report Diagram

Not to Scale                                                    N ↑

LOCATION of CRASH

Point of Impact (POI)

Measurements from fixed reference point

# POLICE CRASH REPORT

Page _____ of _____

| Date of Crash | Time of Crash | Date & Time Crash Reported | Crash # | |
|---|---|---|---|---|

| Collision Location: | Direction of Travel |
|---|---|

| Crash Scene Property Owner's Name: |
|---|

| Unit #/Veh # | Circle One: Driver, Pedestrian, Other Participant | | Sex | Race | Name | |
|---|---|---|---|---|---|---|
| DOB | Home Address | | | | | |
| State of ID | ID # | | | | Type of ID | |
| Vehicle Make & Model | | Vehicle Year | License Plate # | State of Plate | | Year expires |
| VIN | | | | | | |
| Vehicle Owner's Name | | Vehicle Owner's Address | | | | |
| Trailer Make & Model | | Year | License Plate # | State of Plate | VIN | |
| Trailer Owner's Name | | Trailer Owner's Address | | | | |
| Cargo Owner's Name | | Cargo Owner's Address | | | | |
| Describe Cargo Damaged | | | | | | |

| Estimate of Total $ Value of **Crash** Damage<br><br>☐ < $1,000      ☐ $1,000-$5,000<br><br>☐ $5,001 - $10,000   ☐ > $10,000 | Estimate of Total $ Value of **Cargo** Damage<br><br>☐ < $1,000      ☐ $1,000-$5,000<br><br>☐ $5,001 - $10,000   ☐ > $10,000 |
|---|---|
| Name of Witness (not involved in crash) | Address of Witness |
| | |

| Name of individual cited | Offense | Code |
|---|---|---|
| | | |

# POLICE CRASH REPORT   Page _____ of _____

Crash #

**OCCUPANTS (OTHER THAN DRIVERS ALREADY LISTED)**

|   | Vehicle # | Race | Sex | DOB | Name | Address |
|---|-----------|------|-----|-----|------|---------|
| 1 |           |      |     |     |      |         |
| 2 |           |      |     |     |      |         |
| 3 |           |      |     |     |      |         |
| 4 |           |      |     |     |      |         |

Occupant # __  Position        **Front**

☐ trailer

☐ unknown

**Back**

Occupant # __  Position        **Front**

☐ *trailer*

☐ *unknown*

*Back*

Occupant # __  Position        **Front**

☐ trailer

☐ unknown

**Back**

Occupant # __  Position        **Front**

☐ *trailer*

☐ *unknown*

*Back*

**Vehicle # __ Initial Impact**   **Front**

☐ undercarriage

☐ trailer

☐ none

☐ unknown

**Back**

---

**Vehicle # __ Damage**   *Front*

☐ undercarriage

☐ trailer

☐ none

☐ unknown

*Back*

---

*Vehicle # __ Initial Impact*   **Front**

☐ undercarriage

☐ trailer

☐ none

☐ unknown

**Back**

---

*Vehicle # __ Damage*   *Front*

☐ undercarriage

☐ trailer

☐ none

☐ unknown

*Back*

---

**Vehicle # __ Initial Impact**   **Front**

☐ undercarriage

☐ trailer

☐ none

☐ unknown

**Back**

---

**Vehicle # __ Damage**   *Front*

☐ undercarriage

☐ trailer

☐ none

☐ unknown

*Back*

# POLICE CRASH REPORT

Page _____ of _____

Crash #

## Type of Roadway

☐ one-way one-lane        ☐ two-way undivided lanes

☐ private drive           ☐ alley

☐ one-way multi-lanes     ☐ two-way divided lanes

☐ business parking lot    ☐ other _____

## Road Surface

☐ Asphalt    ☐ Concrete    ☐ Chip and Seal    ☐ Dirt    ☐ Gravel

☐ Other _____

## Weather Conditions (Check all that apply)

☐ Sunny    ☐ Overcast       ☐ Foggy    ☐ Smog          ☐ Smoke    ☐ Rain

☐ Hail     ☐ Sleet          ☐ Snow     ☐ Strong winds   ☐ Dry      ☐ Icy Road

☐ Other _____

## Attachments:

☐ witness statements

☐ impound forms _____

☐ other _____

# POLICE CRASH REPORT

Page _____ of _____

Crash #

---

**Vehicle # _____     Type of vehicle**

☐ passenger car     ☐ pickup truck     ☐ motor cycle     ☐ tractor/tractor trailer     ☐ bus

☐ moped          ☐ farm vehicle     ☐ motor home     ☐ recreational veh.     ☐ other _____

**Pre-Crash Vehicle Action**

☐ parked     ☐ passing/overtaking     ☐ changing lanes     ☐ avoiding object in road     ☐ turning

☐ going straight     ☐ slowing or stopped     ☐ starting in traffic     ☐ unattended moving vehicle

☐ merging     ☐ crossing the median     ☐ driving left of center     ☐ backing     ☐ other _____

**If a collision crash: Initial Impact with (fill in one)**

☐ another motor vehicle     ☐ deer     ☐ animal other than deer     ☐ pedestrian     ☐ bicycle

☐ impact attenuator     ☐ guardrail     ☐ median barrier     ☐ utility pole     ☐ bridge

☐ work zone equip.     ☐ mail box     ☐ embankment     ☐ sign     ☐ tree

☐ railway vehicle     ☐ curb     ☐ fence/wall /post     ☐ ditch     ☐ other _____

**If non-collision crash (fill in one)**

☐ jackknife     ☐ overturn/rollover     ☐ fire/explosion     ☐ immersion

☐ cargo shift     ☐ fell from vehicle     ☐ other _____

**Safety equipment Used**

☐ no restraint     ☐ helmet     ☐ restraint belt     ☐ air bag     ☐ child restraint     ☐ unknown

**Safety equipment Effective**     ☐ yes     ☐ no     ☐ not applicable

---

71

# POLICE CRASH REPORT    Page _____ of _____

Crash #

## Vehicle # _____    Type of vehicle

□ passenger car    □ pickup truck    □ motor cycle    □ tractor/tractor trailer    □ bus

□ moped    □ farm vehicle    □ motor home    □ recreational veh.    □ other _____

## Pre-Crash Vehicle Action

□ parked    □ passing/overtaking    □ changing lanes    □ avoiding object in road    □ turning

□ going straight    □ slowing or stopped    □ starting in traffic    □ unattended moving vehicle

□ merging    □ crossing the median    □ driving left of center    □ backing    □ other _____

## If a collision crash: Initial Impact with (fill in one)

□ another motor vehicle    □ deer    □ animal other than deer    □ pedestrian    □ bicycle

□ impact attenuator    □ guardrail    □ median barrier    □ utility pole    □ bridge

□ work zone equip.    □ mail box    □ embankment    □ sign    □ tree

□ railway vehicle    □ curb    □ fence/wall /post    □ ditch    □ other _____

## If non-collision crash (fill in one)

□ jackknife    □ overturn/rollover    □ fire/explosion    □ immersion

□ cargo shift    □ fell from vehicle    □ other _____

## Safety equipment Used

□ no restraint    □ helmet    □ restraint belt    □ air bag    □ child restraint    □ unknown

**Safety equipment Effective**    □ yes    □ no    □ not applicable

# POLICE CRASH REPORT

Page _____ of _____

Crash #

---

**(Complete only if there was an injury and EMS arrived at the Scene)**

**Vehicle # _____**       **EMS # _____**

☐ fatal   ☐ non-fatal serious   ☐ minor   ☐ none   ☐ refused assessment   ☐ unknown

**Nature of Most Severe Injury**

☐ severed   ☐ internal   ☐ burn   ☐ minor bleeding   ☐ bruise   ☐ complaint of pain

☐ other _____

**Location of Most Severe Injury**

☐ head/face/eyes   ☐ neck   ☐ chest   ☐ back   ☐ abdomen   ☐ arms/legs

☐ whole body   ☐ other _____

---

**(Complete only if there was an injury and EMS arrived at the Scene)**

**Vehicle # _____**       **EMS # _____**

☐ fatal   ☐ non-fatal serious   ☐ minor   ☐ none   ☐ refused assessment   ☐ unknown

**Nature of Most Severe Injury**

☐ severed   ☐ internal   ☐ burn   ☐ minor bleeding   ☐ bruise   ☐ complaint of pain

☐ other _____

**Location of Most Severe Injury**

☐ head/face/eyes   ☐ neck   ☐ chest   ☐ back   ☐ abdomen   ☐ arms/legs

☐ whole body   ☐ other _____

# POLICE CRASH REPORT

Page _____ of _____

Crash #

Narrative: _____

_____

_____

_____

_____

_____

_____

_____

_____

_____

_____

_____

_____

_____

_____

_____

_____

_____

_____

_____

_____

_____

_____

_____

_____

_____

_____

| **Crash Diagram** |
|:---:|
|  |

| Officer's Name (printed) | Officer's Signature & Badge # | Date | Approved by Supervisor |
|---|---|---|---|
|  |  |  | □ Yes  □ No |

# Vehicle Crash Proof of Insurance Form

Crash ID _____  _____  In order to avoid having your driver's license suspended, return this completed form signed by your insurance agent within 30 days to _____ Police Department Crash Records.

| Month   Day   Year | Day of Week | Local Time | Vehicles Involved | Injured | Dead |
|---|---|---|---|---|---|
| County where crash occurred | | | Nearest City | | |

| Did crash occur inside city limits?  ◊ yes    ◊ no | Distance and direction from city limits _____  ◊ N  ◊ NE  ◊ NW  ◊ S  ◊ SE  ◊ SW  ◊ E  ◊ W |
|---|---|

Road where crash occurred _____

| Driver 1 | Driver 2 |
|---|---|
| Address | Address |

| Date of Birth | License State | License Type | Date of Birth | License State | License Type |
|---|---|---|---|---|---|

| Driver's License | Driver's License |
|---|---|
| Vehicle Owner's Name | Vehicle Owner's Name |
| Vehicle Owner's Address | Vehicle Owner's Address |

| Vehicle year | Make | Model | Color | Vehicle year | Make | Model | Color |
|---|---|---|---|---|---|---|---|
| License Plate | State | Expiration date | | License Plate | State | Expiration date | |

| | Agency Name | Insurance Policy | Phone |
|---|---|---|---|
| D1 Insurance Company | Agency Name | Insurance Policy | Phone |
| D2 Insurance Company | Agency Name | Insurance Policy | Phone |

| Police Officer Name & Badge | Police Department | Phone |
|---|---|---|
| Insurance Agent Signature | Agent Represents (Check Box)    ☐ Driver 1    ☐ Driver 2 | |

# Vehicle Crash Proof of Insurance Form

Crash ID _____ _____ In order to avoid having your driver's license suspended, return this completed form signed by your insurance agent within 30 days to _____ Police Department Crash Records.

| Month    Day    Year | Day of Week | Local Time | Vehicles Involved | Injured | Dead |
|---|---|---|---|---|---|
| County where crash occurred | | Nearest City | | | |
| Did crash occur inside city limits?  ◊ yes    ◊ no | | Distance and direction from city limits _____  ◊ N ◊ NE ◊ NW ◊ S ◊ SE ◊ SW ◊ E ◊ W | | | |
| Road where crash occurred _____ | | | | | |

| Driver 1 | | | |
|---|---|---|---|
| Address | | | |
| Date of Birth | License State | License Type | |
| Driver's License | | | |
| Vehicle Owner's Name | | | |
| Vehicle Owner's Address | | | |
| Vehicle year | Make | Model | Color |
| License Plate | State | Expiration date | |

| Driver 2 | | | |
|---|---|---|---|
| Address | | | |
| Date of Birth | License State | License Type | |
| Driver's License | | | |
| Vehicle Owner's Name | | | |
| Vehicle Owner's Address | | | |
| Vehicle year | Make | Model | Color |
| License Plate | State | Expiration date | |

| D1 Insurance Company | Agency Name | Insurance Policy | Phone |
|---|---|---|---|
| D2 Insurance Company | Agency Name | Insurance Policy | Phone |

| Police Officer Name & Badge | Police Department | Phone |
|---|---|---|
| Insurance Agent Signature | Agent Represents (Check Box)    ☐ Driver 1    ☐ Driver 2 | |

# Crash Information Exchange Form

This form may be used for crashes that total less than $1,000 worth of damage and when no police report is requested or required. Instead of using this form, either party may request a crash report to be completed by the police at the time of the crash. This form may be used to facilitate your handling of the crash and to exchange driver and vehicle information.

Your (driver's) name: _____

Your (driver's) address: _____

Your (driver's) phone __ _____

Your license plate registration:  State _____  Number _____ Expiration year _____

Your driver's license:  State _____ Number _____

Description of your vehicle:  Make _____ Model _____ Year ____ Color _____

Owner of said vehicle: _____

Address of vehicle owner: _____

Insurance and other information: _____


Location of crash (street)_____

County: _____ State _____

Date of crash _____Time of crash _____

Investigating Officer _____ Badge_____ _____ Phone __ _____

# Vehicle Crash Summary Involving Serious Injury or Fatality

| Crash ID |
| --- |

| Type of Accident ◊ Serious Injury ◊ Fatality Injured __ Fatality __ | | | | Date | Time |
| --- | --- | --- | --- | --- | --- |
| State | County | Closest City | Location of Crash (road) | | |
| Vehicle | Year | Make | Model | Direction of Travel | On (road) |
| Amount of Damage | | Road Condition | | Type of Road | |
| Driver | | Age | Home Address | Sex | Race |
| Driver injured ◊ Yes ◊ No | | Admitted ◊ Yes ◊ No | | Hospital Taken To | |
| Relatives Notified ◊ Yes ◊ No | | Name of Person Notified | | How Related to Driver | |
| Seatbelt/Helmet in Use ◊ Yes ◊ No | ◊ Belt ◊ Helmet | ◊ Did ◊ Did not | | ◊ Reduce ◊ Prevent | ◊ Injuries ◊ Fatality |
| Person other than driver injured ◊ Yes ◊ No | | Admitted ◊ Yes ◊ No | | Hospital Taken To | |
| Name of Person Injured | | Age | Home Address | Sex | Race |
| Relatives Notified ◊ Yes ◊ No | | | Name of Person Notified | How Related to Patient | |
| Seatbelt/Helmet in Use ◊ Yes ◊ No | ◊ Belt ◊ Helmet | ◊ Did ◊ Did not | | ◊ Reduce ◊ Prevent | ◊ Injuries ◊ Fatality |

| Person arrested | Most serious charge | | |
| --- | --- | --- | --- |
| Investigating officer's name (printed) | Investigating officer's signature | Badge | Phone |
| Police Department | Police Department Address | | Date |

79

# POLICE VEHICLE CRASH FORM

| Date of Crash | Time of Crash | County | Location of Crash |
|---|---|---|---|
| Type of Crash<br><br>(check all that apply)<br><br>◊ Property Damage<br><br>◊ Personal Injury | **Weather Conditions**<br><br>◊ Clear    ◊ Freezing Rain<br><br>◊ Cloudy    ◊ Sleet<br><br>◊ Fog/Smoke    ◊ Snow<br><br>◊ Rain    ◊ Other | **Lighting Conditions**<br><br>◊ Daylight<br><br>◊ Dawn/Dusk<br><br>◊ Dark with lights<br><br>◊ Dark with no lights | Road Conditions<br><br>(check all that apply)<br><br>◊ straight    ◊ Wet<br><br>◊ Curve    ◊ Concrete<br><br>◊ Hill    ◊ Asphalt<br><br>◊ Slippery    ◊ Gravel<br><br>◊ Dry    ◊ Other |

| **Department Vehicle** | | **Other Vehicle** | |
|---|---|---|---|
| Driver's last name | Driver's first name | Driver's last name | Driver's first name |
| Home Address | | Home Address | |
| Date of Birth | Sex   Phone # | Date of Birth | Sex   Phone # |
| Driver's License # | State of Issue | Driver's License # | State of Issue |

| **Department Vehicle Information** | | | | **Other Vehicle Information** | | | |
|---|---|---|---|---|---|---|---|
| Lic. Plate # | Issuing State | Vehicle year | Color | Lic. Plate # | Issuing State | Vehicle year | Color |
| # of Occupants | Vehicle Towed<br><br>◊ Yes ◊ No | Direction of Travel | Posted Speed | # of Occupants | Vehicle Towed<br><br>◊ Yes ◊ No | Direction of Travel | Posted Speed |

## Injuries

| Name | Address | Injury | Age | Sex | Code |
|------|---------|--------|-----|-----|------|
|      |         |        |     |     |      |
|      |         |        |     |     |      |
|      |         |        |     |     |      |

Code: V1 = vehicle 1; V2 = vehicle 2; P = pedestrian; B = bicyclist; O = other

Draw a diagram of the crash.

↑N

Describe the event.

| Officer's Name (printed) | Officer's Signature & Badge # | Date | Approved by Supervisor |
|---------------------------|-------------------------------|------|------------------------|
|                           |                               |      | ☐ Yes  ☐ No            |

# REPORT OF POLICE CAR CRASH OR EQUIPMENT LOSS

| Name of Employee | Badge | Date of Damage/Loss | Time of Damage/Loss |
|---|---|---|---|
| ◊ Police Car Crash    ◊ Equipment Damage | | ◊ In Line of Duty | |
| ◊ Other Police Car Damage    ◊ Equipment Loss | | ◊ Not in Line of Duty | |
| Location of Crash/Loss | | | |

## Police Car Crash

| License | Make | Model | Year | Mileage | Assigned To |
|---|---|---|---|---|---|
| ◊ Emergency Run   ◊ Normal Driving   ◊ Backing   ◊Parked | | | | | Hrs. on Duty |
| ◊ Red/Blue Lights On   ◊Siren On | | | | | |
| Names of Employee Injured | | | | | |
| Name & Address of Other Involved Party | | | | | |
| Insurance Company of Other Involved Party | | | | Policy | |

## Police Vehicle Damage Repair Estimates

| Garage   1 | Cost |
|---|---|
| Garage   2 | Cost |
| Garage   3 | Cost |

## Police Equipment Damaged

| Item | Serial # | Status Code |
|---|---|---|
| | | __ Lost/Stolen __ Destroyed __ Damaged/Repaired __ Other |
| | | __ Lost/Stolen __ Destroyed __ Damaged/Repaired __ Other |

Affidavit: I affirm that, to the best of my knowledge, the information on this form is true.

Signature of Responsible Officer _____ Date _____

Page____of_____ Type of Report _____ Report _____

## *Interview Statement*

_____
_____
_____
_____
_____
_____
_____
_____
_____
_____
_____
_____
_____
_____
_____
_____
_____
_____
_____
_____
_____
_____
_____

*Draw a diagonal line through all unused space.*

| Print Name | Signature | Date/Time |
|---|---|---|

Witness_____ Signature_____
       Print name

Witness_____ Signature_____
       Print name

# VOLUNTARY STATEMENT This is page _____ of ___.

_____ Police Department

Date_____ Place _____ time started _____

I, _____, am _____ years of age, being born on _____ have

been warned by _____, with the _____
police department, that I do not have to make any statement at all, nor answer any questions. I was also warned
and advised of my right to a lawyer of my own choice before or at any time during questioning, and if I am not
able to hire a lawyer, I may request to have a lawyer appointed to me. I do not now want a lawyer, and I waive
my right to the advice and presence of a lawyer, knowing that anything I say can and will be used against me in
a court of law. I now want to make a statement.

_____

_____

_____

_____

_____

_____

_____

_____

_____

_____

_____

_____

*Draw a diagonal line through all unused space. Have person place initials at end of statement.*

**This form was completed at (time) _____.**

**Signature of person providing statement _____**

Witness_____          Signature_____          Badge _____
          Print name

Witness_____          Signature_____          Badge _____
          Print name

# POLICE DEPARTMENT PUBLIC SAFETY CHECKPOINT PLAN

APPOVED PLAN REQUIRED WHEN AGENCY PERSONNEL PLANS TO PARTICIPATE IN OR ASSISTS OTHER AGENCIES.

DATE:_____  START TIME:_____  END TIME:_____

LOCATION:_____

*SITE CONSIDERATIONS*:

____THE LOCATION SELECTED FOR A PUBLIC SAFETY CHECKPOINT IS BASED ON THE SIGNIFICANCE OF A PUBLIC SAFETY PROBLEM IN AN AREA.  DESCRIBE REASON THE PROPOSED SITE WAS SELECTED FOR A PUBLIC SAFETY CHECKPOINT.

_____

_____

_____

____ THE CHECKPOINT LOCATION WILL BE VISIBLE BY APPROACHING MOTORISTS FROM A SAFE DISTANCE.

____THE CHECKPOINT WILL NOT BE SET UP IN A CURVE, OVER THE CREST OF A HILL OR OTHER DANGEROUS LOCATION.

____THE TRAFFIC FLOW WILL NOT BE ALLOWED TO BACK UP SO MUCH THAT IT BECOMES A HAZARD.

____IF ADDITIONAL OFFICERS AND PRECAUTIONS ARE REQUIRED WHEN SETTING UP THE CHECKPOINT ON A FOUR-LANE

ROAD OR AT A FOUR-WAY INTERSECTION, PROVISIONS WILL BE MADE.

____THE SITE WILL INCLUDE ADEQUATE SPACE ON THE ROADSIDE TO MOVE VEHICLES THAT MAY BE CITED, AN ARREST IS TO BE MADE, OR FURTHER INVESTIGATION IS REQUIRED.

## *PURPOSE*:

CHECKPOINT WILL BE USED TO FOCUS ENFORCEMENT EFFORTS IN THE FOLLOWING AREAS (CHECK ALL THAT APPLY):

___DETECTING IMPAIRED DRIVERS

___INSPECTING DRIVERS' LICENSES AND REGISTRATIONS

___APPREHENDING FLEEING FUGITIVES WHO ARE LIKELY TO FLEE BY WAY OF PARTICULAR ROUTE

___THWARTING AN IMMINENT TERRORIST ATTACK

## MANPOWER

DETAIL MUST INCLUDE A MINIMUM OF FOUR OFFICERS, INCLUDING A FIELD SUPERVISOR AT THE CHECKPOINT AT ALL TIMES.

SUPERVISOR ON SCENE:_____

OFFICER & BADGĚ :_____ OFFICER & BADGĚ :_____

OFFICER & BADGĚ :_____ OFFICER & BADGĚ :_____

## OTHER AGENCY PRESENT AT THE CHECKPOINT

AGENCY NAME:_____ OFFICER NAME & BADGĚ :_____

### OTHER AGENCY PRESENT AT THE CHECKPOINT

AGENCY NAME:_____ OFFICER NAME & BADGĚ :_____

## WARNING AND SAFETY

____ "PUBLIC SAFETY CHECKPOINT AHEAD" SIGNS WILL BE PLACED AT A SAFE & PRUDENT DISTANCE FROM CHECKPOINT.

____TRAFFIC CONES OR BARRICADES WILL BE USED TO ENHANCE THE VISIBILITY OF THE CHECKPOINT.

____ALL UNIFORMED OFFICERS ASSIGNED TO THE OPERATION WILL WEAR UNIFORMS AND REFLECTIVE TRAFFIC VESTS.

____PLAIN CLOTHES OFFICERS WILL DISPLAY POLICE IDs AT ALL TIMES DURING THE CHECKPOINT OPERATIONS.

____ALL VEHICLES USED FOR TRAFFIC CONTROL WILL BE MARKED PATROL VEHICLES.

## CHECKPOINT OPERATIONS:

____ A SYSTEM WILL BE USED TO SELECT VEHICLES AT THE CHECKPOINT LOCATION.  FOR EXAMPLE, ALL VEHICLES OR EVERY FIFTH VEHICLE WILL BE STOPPED.  AT NO TIME WILL RANDOM STOPS BE UTILIZED.

____ DURING OPERATIONS, OFFICERS WILL APPROACH EACH MOTORIST AND EXPLAIN THE PURPOSE OF THE STOP.

____ ALL PUBLIC SAFETY CHECKPOINT OPERATIONS WILL BE VIDEOTAPED.

## NIGHTTIME REQUIEMENTS

___ALL "PUBLIC SAFETY CHECKPOINT AHEAD" SIGNS WILL BE ILLUMINATED FOR THE DURATION OF THE CHECKPOINT.

___NIGHTTIME CHECKPOINT OFFICERS WILL WEAR UNIFORMS, REFLECTIVE TRAFFIC VESTS AND UTILIZE FLASHLIGHTS WITH TRAFFIC WANDS.

___PLAIN CLOTHES OFFICERS WILL DISPLAY POLICE IDs AT ALL TIMES DURING THE CHECKPOINT OPERATIONS.

___THE PUBLIC SAFETY CHECKPOINT WILL BE ILLUMINATED IN A MANNER THAT WILL ENSURE THAT ANY APPROACHING MOTORIST HAS ADEQUATE WARNING OF THE CHECKPOINT. (EMERGENCY OVERHEAD LIGHTING ON POLICE VEHICLES SHOULD NOT BE RELIED UPON TO PROVIDE SUCH ILLUMINATION.)

## SUPERVISOR APPROVALS:

CHECKPOINT APPROVAL:_____DATE:_____

## CHECKPOINT ACTIVITY SUMMARY

DUI ARREST_____     ALCO-SENSOR TESTS _____     DATAMASTER TESTS _____

SUSPENDED LICENSES_____     UNINSURED MOTORISTS_____

REGISTRATION VIOLATIONS_____     SAFETY BELT VIOLATIONS_____

CHILD SAFETY SEAT_____     DRUG ARREST_____     OTHER_____

# Special Activity Report

District _____ OIC _____ Date _____

Start time _____ End time _____

Location _____

□ Self-Initiated
□ Assigned by Department

## Type of Support (check all that apply)

□ City Police          □ Radar
□ County Police        □ Vascar
□ State Police         □ Air
                       □ Ghost Car

## Focus of Special Activity

□ Speed               □ DUI
□ Seatbelts           □ Drug Interdiction
□ Work Zone           □ Commercial Motor Vehicle

# Activity

| | | | |
|---|---|---|---|
| Total Traffic Citations | | Total Traffic Warnings | |
| Speeding Citations | | Speeding Warnings | |
| Seatbelt Citations | | Seatbelt Warnings | |
| Child Restraint Citations | | Child Restraint Warnings | |
| Crash Related Citations | | Crashes Investigated | |
| DUI Arrests | | Intelligence Reports | |
| Minor Consuming Arrests | | Commercial Motor Vehicle Citations | |
| Other Alcohol Arrests | | Commercial Motor Vehicle Warnings | |
| Criminal Arrests | | Alco-sensor tests | |
| Drug related Arrests | | DataMaster Tests | |
| Work Zone Citations | | Police Services | |

| Car Number of Each Unit Assigned | Badge of Each Unit | Time Started | Time Ended | Mileage |
|---|---|---|---|---|
| | | | | |
| | | | | |
| | | | | |
| | | | | |
| | | | | |

Total of Units _____ Total Man Hours _____ Total Mileage _____

# DUI Investigative Notes

**(Intended solely for practicing Field Sobriety Tests; there is no claim to the significance or validity of the tests. However, there must be some reference level to determine if a suspect has passed or failed each test.)**

# Field Sobriety Directions

## Walk-and-turn

Have the suspect place his left foot on the line and his right foot in front of his left (heel to toe)

Have the suspect stand in this position, demonstrate and explain the test before he begins

**Take nine steps**

**Stay on line**

**Count the steps out loud**

**Watch your feet**

**Once you start, do not stop**

**Keep hands at side**

**During turn, swivel on left foot and take small steps with right foot to turn around**

**After the turn, take 9 steps and return to the starting point in the same fashion.**

Do you understand? Begin.

# One-leg stand

Have the suspect stand with his heels together and his arms at his side

Have the suspect stand in this position, demonstrate and explain the test before he begins

**Lift your foot (either foot) 6" off of the ground**

**Keep your leg straight in front of you**

**Watch your foot**

**Keep your arms at you side**

**Count out loud up to 30**

**Count 1001, 1002, 1003, 1004,….**

Do you understand? Begin.

# Horizontal Nystagmus

Face toward me and do not turn your head; only move your eyes

Follow my finger with your eyes

[Move finger from side to side; move finger so that eyes can be assessed at 45 degrees and at maximum deviation; record eye movements]

# Finger Count

Count from 1 to 4, touching the tip of your thumb to the tip of your fingers

Count from pinky to index finger, then index finger to pinky

Count 1, 2, 3, 4, 4, 3, 2, 1

Do you understand? Begin.

# Backward Count

Example: Tell suspect to count backward from 33 to 14

# Alphabet:

Ask suspect if he knows alphabet

Ask the suspect to indicate his level of education

Ask suspect to recite alphabet (but not to sing it)

# Alco-sensor test

Place the breath tube on the instrument

Press read button to indicate that no measurement is currently on the instrument

Press set button to set instrument

Place tube in suspect's mouth

Place hand behind tube to measure breath

Tell suspect to blow into breath tube

Tell suspect you want a steady breath and for him to blow until you tell him to stop

After several seconds, press read button to take a reading

Determine reading (a reading will automatically come up or can press read button)

Toggle set and read buttons and swing instrument to clear out current readings

# Horizontal Nystagmus

## Horizontal Nystagmus Test Results  ◊ **Passed** ◊ **Failed**

**If suspect exhibited 4 or more clues, then it is a failed test.**

6 total clues of impairment - 3 for each eye

1. Lack of Smooth Pursuit
2. Distinct Nystagmus at Maximum Deviation
3. Onset of Nystagmus Prior to 45 degrees (includes Nystagmus while eyes at rest)

**Horizontal Nystagmus Test** (check box only if characteristic observed)       Left     Right

   ◊ Lack of Smooth Pursuit                                         \_\_\_\_  \_\_\_\_

   ◊ Distinct Nystagmus at Maximum Deviation              \_\_\_\_  \_\_\_\_

   ◊ Onset of Nystagmus Prior to 45 degrees (includes while eyes at rest)  \_\_\_\_  \_\_\_\_

## <u>Tests to detect head injuries</u> (if check yes, then the test is suspect)

     Eyes have Equal Tracking         ◊ Yes ◊ No ◊ Does not apply

     Eyes have Equal Size Pupils      ◊ Yes ◊ No ◊ Does not apply

# Walk-and-Turn

## Walk-and-Turn  Test Results          ◊ Passed  ◊ Failed

## If suspect exhibited 2 or more clues, then it is a failed test.

8 clues of impairment

1. Cannot maintain balance during Instructions stage
2. Starts too soon
3. Stops while walking
4. Misses heel-to-toe ½ inch or more between steps
5. Steps off of the line
6. Raises arms 6" or more
7. Turns improperly
8. Takes wrong number of steps

|   |   | R9 | L8 | R7 | L6 | R5 | L4 | R3 | L2 | R1 | ← |
|---|---|----|----|----|----|----|----|----|----|----|----|
| L | R | L1 | R2 | L3 | R4 | L5 | R6 | L7 | R8 | L9 | → |

## Walk-and-Turn

### INSTRUCTIONS STAGE

Keeps balance     ◊ Yes   ◊ No

Starts too soon   ◊ Yes   ◊ No

| **WALKING STAGE** | **First Nine Steps** | **Second Nine Steps** |
|---|---|---|
| Stops Walking | _____ | _____ |
| Misses Heel-to-toe | _____ | _____ |
| Steps off of line | _____ | _____ |
| Raises Arms > 6" | _____ | _____ |
| Actual Number of Steps Taken | _____ | _____ |

Improper turn (describe) _____

Cannot perform Test (Explain) _____

Other: _____

# One Leg Stand

## One Leg Stand  Test Results          ◊ Passed  ◊ Failed

**If suspect exhibited 2 or more clues, then it is a failed test.**

4 clues of impairment

1. Sways while balancing
2. Raises arms more than 6"
3. Hops
4. Puts foot down

Puts foot down 3 times is a failed test.    Foot stood on  ____ L    ____ R

| Check (if yes) | Performance |
|---|---|
|  | Sways while balancing |
|  | Raises arms more than 6" |
|  | Hops |
|  | Puts foot down |

Puts foot down 3 times (failed test)     ◊ Yes  ◊ No

Type of footwear_____

Cannot perform test (explain)_____

_____

Other_____

_____

# Backward Count

**Backward Count Test Results**       ◊ **Passed  ◊ Failed**

**If suspect exhibited 2 or more clues, then it is a failed test.**

3 clues of impairment

◊ Hesitation

◊ Incomplete (Left out numbers) _____

◊ Continued past number and counted to_____

◊ Other _____

Asked participant to count from _____ to _____.

# Alphabet A-Z

## Alphabet (A-Z) Test Results     ◊ **Passed** ◊ **Failed**

**If suspect exhibited 2 or more clues, then it is a failed test.**

4 clues of impairment

◊ Left out letters:_____

◊ Hesitated

◊ Incomplete

◊ Sang Alphabet

◊ Other (describe)_____

# Finger Count

**Finger Count Test Results**       ◊ **Passed** ◊ **Failed**

**If suspect exhibited 2 or more clues, then it is a failed test.**

4 clues of impairment

◊ Hesitation

◊ Misses tip of thumb to tip of finger

◊ Does not count 1-2-3-4-4-3-2-1

◊ Count not in alignment with appropriate finger

◊ Other _____

# IMPLIED CONSENT WARNING

I have probable cause to believe that you have operated a vehicle while intoxicated.  I must now offer to you the opportunity to submit to a chemical test, and inform you that your refusal to submit to a chemical test will result in the suspension of your driving privileges for ___ months.

Will you now take a chemical test?

Some departments arrest at this point. There is probable cause.  Other departments arrest after the DataMaster test.  In the latter case, the additional evidence gained by the DataMaster test is considered part of the totality of circumstance (a refusal will result in an arrest because there is probable cause).

# DataMaster Evidence Ticket

Below is information that is recorded on a DataMaster evidence ticket.

State of _____

Instrument _____

Date: _____

Subject name _____

DOB _____

SSN _____

Operator's name _____

Department _____

**Breath Analysis**

Calibration/Self Tests ____ passed ____ failed

Subject's sample ____ passed ___ failed ____refused    BrAC %____

Start Observation Time _____    Time of DataMaster Test _____

Operator's name _____ Signature _____ Badge ____

# Affidavit for Probable Cause: Driving While Intoxicated

State of _____ in the _____ Court in the County of _____

State of _____

        vs.

_____

_____

I, _____, a law enforcer with the _____ Department, swear that on the

_____ day of _____ 20__, at about _____ ☐am ☐ pm (Name) _____, the accused, a

(race) _____ , (sex) ☐ male ☐ female, (date of birth) _____, was observed at (location) _____

_____ in _____ County, _____ (State) operating a motor

vehicle (description) _____.

The accused, having ☐ _____ (State) driver's license ☐ social security number ☐ other identification number

(list number) _____ operated a motor vehicle under the following circumstances:

## Preliminary Observations

☐ I observed the accused operate the motor vehicle in my presence.

☐ _____ observed the accused operate a motor vehicle.

☐ I had reason to believe that the accused operated a motor vehicle because _____

☐ The accused committed the following traffic violations:_____

☐ On private property, the accused's driving was erratic and unusual because _____

## Reason for the Traffic Investigation

☐ The accused committed the following traffic violations: _____

☐ The accused was already stopped when I approached.

☐ Other:_____

# Crash?

Was there a crash involved? ☐ no ☐ yes      Number of vehicles involved in crash _____

☐ I witnessed the accused's crash.

☐ _____ witnessed the crash and identified the accused as a driver involved in the crash.

☐ The accused admitted to being the driver involved in the crash.

☐ The result of the crash was ☐ property damage _____ ☐ personal injury (name) _____

# Field Observations

I had probable cause to believe that the accused was intoxicated because I observed (check all that apply):

| | | |
|---|---|---|
| ☐ Odor of alcoholic beverage | ☐ alcohol beverage containers in view | ☐ admitted consuming alcohol |
| ☐ blood shot eyes | ☐ improperly left vehicle in gear | ☐ leaned against vehicle |
| ☐ slurred Speech | ☐ failed to shut off vehicle at crash scene | ☐ soiled/disorderly clothing |
| ☐ poor manual dexterity | ☐ was involved in crash | ☐ could not open door |
| ☐ poor balance | ☐ could not exit vehicle on own | ☐ fell asleep at scene |
| ☐ belligerent attitude | ☐ staggered from vehicle | ☐ excessive giggling |

# Field Sobriety Tests (check all of the tests that were administered and the corresponding results)

☐ Horizontal Nystagmus      ☐ Passed      ☐ Failed

☐ Walk-and-turn      ☐ Passed      ☐ Failed

☐ One-leg stand      ☐ Passed      ☐ Failed

☐ Finger count      ☐ Passed      ☐ Failed

☐ Backward count      ☐ Passed      ☐ Failed _____ (list range & describe response)

☐ Alphabet      ☐ Passed      ☐ Failed _____ (describe response)

☐ Rhomberg balance      ☐ Passed      ☐ Failed

☐ Finger-to-nose      ☐ Passed      ☐ Failed

☐ Other      ☐ Passed      ☐ Failed _____ (describe test)

☐ Alco-sensor 0._____ grams of alcohol per 210 liters of breath.      ☐ Passed      ☐ Failed

101

# Chemical Test

☐ I informed the accused of the state implied consent law & the accused ☐submitted to ☐ refused

   the chemical test.

☐ The accused was unable to take the chemical test because ☐ injured ☐ unconscious ☐ too intoxicated

☐ _____, a certified chemical test operator, performed a chemical DataMaster test on the accused
at (location) _____. The alcohol concentration was equivalent to 0._____ gram of
alcohol per 210 liters of breath.

☐ I was informed by _____ that a blood test was conducted on accused at _____ ☐ am ☐ pm
and that the result was an alcohol concentration equivalent 0._____ gram of alcohol per 100 milliliters of blood.

☐ I was informed by _____ that a ☐ blood ☐ urine ☐ other test was conducted on
accused at _____ ☐am ☐ pm at (location) _____ and that the result was positive
for the controlled substance _____.

I swear or affirm that under penalty of perjury that the foregoing facts are true.

_____    _____    _____

Signature of Affiant                Date              Print name and Department

# Previous Convictions

I, _____, have examined the accused driving/criminal record and have determined that the
accused has a prior Operating While Intoxicated conviction on (date) _____ from _____ Court in
_____ County, _____ (State) having cause number _____.

I swear or affirm that under penalty of perjury that the foregoing facts are true.

_____    _____

Signature of Affiant                          Date

102

# Receipt for Driver's License (confiscated by police)

_____ Police Department   ORĬ _____

Charges _____

Date of arrest _____ time _____ □ am   □ pm

Driver's license number _____ License state _____

Name _____ DOB _____

Current address _____

Sex _____ Weight _____ Height _____ Eyes _____ Hair _____

The above motorist  □ refused the alcohol test  □ failed  the alcohol test  0._____ %.

County _____

_____ _____ _____ _____
Date                    Department                   Signature of Officer        Badgĕ

# CHARGING FORM FOR DRIVING WHILE INTOXICATED

State of _____          IN THE _____ COURT

County of _____          CAUSE NO. _____


State of _____

vs.

_____

DOB: _____

SSN: _____


**INFORMATION FOR (OFFENSE TITLE):** _____

**CODE** _____          **CLASS** _____          ☐ **MISDEMEANOR**     ☐ **FELONY**

COMES NOW, _____ (name of officer), who being duly sworn upon oath,

says that on or about : (date of offense) _____, 20____, at (location of offense)

_____, in _____ County, ____ (State), one (defendant)

_____ of (Defendant's address) _____

did then and there RECKLESSLY, KNOWINGLY, or INTENTIONALLY: (describe elements of the

crime)

_____

_____

_____

_____

All of which is contrary to the form of the statute in such cases made and provided, and against the peace and dignity of the

State of _____.

**I swear or affirm under penalty of perjury that the foregoing representations are true.**

Date _____ Arresting officer's name (printed) _____

Arresting Officer's Signature & Badge _____

Witness List: _____

Approved by (Prosecutor) _____

# Monthly ALCO-SENSOR Report

_____ Police Department

Officer _____ Badge # _____

| | | Alco-sensor # | County |
|---|---|---|---|

| DATE | LOCATION | ALCO SENSOR | | BREATHALYZER | | CHARGE | REMARKS |
|------|----------|------|--------|------|--------|--------|---------|
| | | TIME | RESULT | TIME | RESULT | | |
| | | | | | | | |
| | | | | | | | |
| | | | | | | | |
| | | | | | | | |
| | | | | | | | |
| | | | | | | | |
| | | | | | | | |
| | | | | | | | |
| | | | | | | | |
| | | | | | | | |
| | | | | | | | |
| | | | | | | | |

# MOBILE VIDEO TAPE LOG

## _____ Police Department

Name:_____ Badge #:_____ Case/Incident #:_____

Primary County: _____ Start Date: _____ End Date: _____

| Date | Time | Name/Subject | UTT/Case/Incident # | Offense | Remarks | County |
|------|------|--------------|---------------------|---------|---------|--------|
|      |      |              |                     |         |         |        |
|      |      |              |                     |         |         |        |
|      |      |              |                     |         |         |        |
|      |      |              |                     |         |         |        |
|      |      |              |                     |         |         |        |
|      |      |              |                     |         |         |        |
|      |      |              |                     |         |         |        |
|      |      |              |                     |         |         |        |
|      |      |              |                     |         |         |        |
|      |      |              |                     |         |         |        |
|      |      |              |                     |         |         |        |
|      |      |              |                     |         |         |        |

# I-94 Arrival/Departure Record (US. Department of Justice, 2002, 1991)

Non-U.S. citizens will have I-94

Green – Visa Waiver

White – Non Visa Waiver

Non-U.S. citizens who are visiting the U.S. will have the bottom part of the I-94, which is written in English.

The I-94 arrival/departure record may be used to identify visitors when they try to present identifications to police officers that are not written in English.

The information below will be provided on the I-94 arrival/departure record and it will be written in English.

**Departure #** _____

**Last Name (family name)** _____

**First name** _____

**DOB** _____

**Country of Citizenship** _____

# INCIDENT REPORTS (NON-CRIMINAL)

# Incident Report (non-criminal)　　Page ___ of ___

| Incident (non-criminal) ˅ | | | |
|---|---|---|---|
| Location of Incident | City | County | State |

Incident :　　Lost Property　　Found Property　　Victim Injured　　Other
　　　　　　　　☐　　　　　　　　☐　　　　　　　☐　　　　　　☐ _____

| Date &Time of Incident | Date &Time Reported to Dispatch | Dispatch Badge # |
|---|---|---|

| Victim Name | Victim's Phone |
|---|---|

| Victim's Address | Victim's DOB | Victim's SSN |
|---|---|---|

| Victim's Sex | Victim's Race | Victim's Place of Treatment (Name & Address) |
|---|---|---|

Person Who Reported Incident (Name)

Person Who Reported Incident (Address)

Witness to Incident (Name)

Witness to Incident (Address)

| Witness: ☐ Driver's License　☐ State ID　　☐ Other _____ | Number | State | DOB |
|---|---|---|---|

Property Record & Receipt #

Weapon, Tool, or Force

| Vehicle Involved?　☐ Yes　☐ No | VIN | Make | Model | Color | Year | License State |
|---|---|---|---|---|---|---|

Name and address of Vehicle Owner

Name, address, and phone # of Wrecker that towed vehicle

| Officer's Name (printed) | Officer's Signature & Badge # | Date | Approved by Supervisor　☐ Yes　☐ No |
|---|---|---|---|

| Incident (non-criminal) ˇ | Page ____ of ____ |
|---|---|

**NARRATIVE**

ATTACHMENTS:

| Officer's Name (printed) | Officer's Signature & Badge # | Date | Approved by Supervisor<br><br>☐ Yes ☐ No |
|---|---|---|---|

# Supplemental Incident Report

| Incident  (non-criminal) | | | |
|---|---|---|---|
| Location of Offense | City | County | State |
| Offense | | | Code |
| Victim Name | | Victim's Phone | |

Summary:

 

 

 

 

 

 

 

 

 

 

 

 

ATTACHMENTS:

| Officer's Name (printed) | Officer's Signature & Badge # | Date | Approved by Supervisor <br><br> ☐ Yes    ☐ No |
|---|---|---|---|
| | | | |

# APPLICATION FOR 72 HOUR MEDICAL DETENTION

STATE OF _____ Incident _____ Date _____

---

**TO:** _____ **COURT OF** _____ **COUNTY,** _____ **(State)**

**IN THE MATTER OF** _____ **, Patient  DOB:** _____ **SEX __MALE __FEMALE**

THE OFFICER HEREIN STATES TO THE COURT THE FOLLOWING:

1. THAT THE PATIENT _____ AGE _____ DOB _____ , RESIDES

AT _____

AND IS NOW AT _____ .

2. THAT THIS OFFICER HAS REASON TO BELIEVE THAT THE RESPONDENT IS MENTALLY DISORDERED AS DEFINED BY LAW AND PRESENTS THE LIKELIHOOD OF SERIOUS HARM TO SELF OR OTHERS, AND THUS IS IN NEED OF DETENTION, EVALUATION AND TREATMENT.

3. THE FACTS THAT SUPPORT THE OFFICER'S BELIEF THAT THE RESPONDANT IS MENTALLY DISORDERED ARE:

4. THE FACTS THAT SUPPORT THE OFFICER'S BELIEF THAT THE RESPONDANT PRESENTS A LIKELIHOOD OF SERIOUS HARM ARE:

5. THIS OFFICER REQUESTS THE COURT TO ORDER THAT THE PATIENT BE HELD IN CUSTODY AND TRANSFERRED TO _____

FOR DETENTION, EVALUATION, AND TREATMENT FOR A PERIOD NOT TO EXCEED 72 HOURS PURSUANT TO LAW.

THIS OFFICER VERIFIES & AFFIRMS THAT THE FACTS STATED IN THIS APPLICATION ARE TRUE.

ATTACHMENT: DOCTOR'S ORDER

| OFFICER'S NAME & BADGE | | DEPARTMENT ADDRESS |
|---|---|---|
| OFFICER'S SIGNATURE | | DEPARTMENT TELEPHONE |
| JUDGE'S NAME | JUDGE'S SIGNATURE | PHONE |

# Police Department's Animal Bite Report

Case Report _____ _____ Incident Location _____

| Report Date | Report Time | Reported by<br><br>Name:<br><br><br>Phone: | Received by | Victim Type (circle 2)<br><br>Human/Animal<br><br>Juvenile/Adult | Date of Bite | Biting animal tested for rabies after bite?<br><br>Y    N<br><br><br><br>Result of test (circle)<br><br>Pos    Neg | Incident<br><br>On  Off<br><br>Personal property |
|---|---|---|---|---|---|---|---|
| | | | | | | | |

| **BITING ANIMAL** | Bat | Cattle | Cat | Chipmunk Squirrel | Dog | Ferret Fox Rabbit Raccoon Snake | Gerbil Hamster | Mouse Rat | Other (specify) |
|---|---|---|---|---|---|---|---|---|---|
| Species of biting animal | | | | | | | | | |

| **VICTIM** | None | Soap & Water | Alcohol or Peroxide | Antibiotics | Wound Stitched |
|---|---|---|---|---|---|
| **TREATMENT OF VICTIM** (check all that apply) | | | | | |

| **VICTIM** | Human Rabies Immune Globulin | Rabies Vaccine | Number of Doses Planned |
|---|---|---|---|
| Rabies Prophylaxis | | | |

| **VICTIM** | Human | Other Domestic Animal | Other Animal (wild) |
|---|---|---|---|
| Victim of Bite (check one) | | | |

| VICTIM | Minor, no break in skin | Minor puncture in skin | Moderate puncture in skin | Severe puncture (deep, crushing, or tears due to shaking) | Death |
|---|---|---|---|---|---|
| Seriousness of Bite (check one) | | | | | |

| BITING ANIMAL | Confined at time of bite (1) | Roaming at time of bite (2) | A N D | Repeat Biter, previous on file (3) | No previous bites on file (4) |
|---|---|---|---|---|---|
| Animal that bit victim (Check either box 1 or 2. Check either box 3 or 4) | | | | | |

| BITING ANIMAL | Aggression | Convulsion | Unable to Eat or Drink | Paralysis | Excessive Salivation |
|---|---|---|---|---|---|
| Behaviors Exhibited by Biting Animal (Check all that apply) | | | | | |

# Vehicle Impound Rules (Department Policy)

## On the Vehicle Impound Form

Document all items over $20.

Document group of items over $20.  For example: *A case containing 20 DVDs.*

Inventory all cash.

Document all damage.  If a car is scratched all over, then indicate that the car is scratched all over.

## Example (on Vehicle Impound Form)

### Inventory

Cash: $44.48

One silver-colored DeMarini aluminum baseball bat, 31"; serial  56848494.

One black Cobra CB radio; serial  T5848930.

### Damage

Cracked windshield.

Dent on front driver side fender.

Scratches all over car.

## In the Narrative of the Vehicle Impound Incident Report

State date, time, and location.  State the date and time that the vehicle was reported abandoned, its location, and the date and time that the wrecker was called.  The time differential must indicate that a violation of law has occurred (e.g., more than 72 hours).

State who arrived at the scene and who removed the vehicle.  Include all times.

# VEHICLE IMPOUND FORM

RETURN THIS PORTION OF COMPLETED FORM TO: BMV/DMV/Secretary of State

Available for release  ☐ Yes  ☐ No _____  Incident ____ _____

| TO BE COMPLETED BY POLICE OFFICER – VEHICLE & LOCATION INFORMATION | | | | | | |
|---|---|---|---|---|---|---|
| CITY | | COUNTY | STREET | | | Date Towed |
| MAKE OF VEHICLE | | YEAR | STYLE | MODEL | COLOR | VIN |
| LICENSE PLATE # | | Year Expired | State | Odometer Reading | | |
| Name of Vehicle Owner Determined by ☐ VIN ☐ Plate ☐ Paper Registration | | Name of Person Last in Possession of Vehicle    ☐ SAME AS OWNER | | | | |
| Name & Address of Owner | | If Not Owner, Address of Person in Last Possession of Vehicle | | | | |
| Name of Arrested | | Charge & Code | | | | |

| TO BE COMPLETED BY POLICE OFFICER – VEHICLE & REASON FOR TOW | | | | | | |
|---|---|---|---|---|---|---|
| **GENERAL CONDITION OF VEHICLE** | | | **TOW IN REQUESTED BY** | | **REASON FOR TOW** | |

**GENERAL CONDITION OF VEHICLE**

| | GOOD | POOR | MISSING |
|---|---|---|---|
| FRAME | ☐ | ☐ | ☐ |
| WINDSHIELD | ☐ | ☐ | ☐ |
| RADIATOR | ☐ | ☐ | ☐ |
| WHEELS | ☐ | ☐ | ☐ |
| TIRES | ☐ | ☐ | ☐ |
| SEATS | ☐ | ☐ | ☐ |
| SHELL | ☐ | ☐ | ☐ |
| SPARE TIRE | ☐ | ☐ | ☐ |
| RADIO | ☐ | ☐ | ☐ |

**TOW IN REQUESTED BY**

___ STATE POLICE
___ COUNTY POLICE
___ STATE CONSTABLE
___ CITY POLICE
___ OTHER

Estimated Value of Vehicle ($)

___0-100  ___101-1000  ___1001-5000

___Over 5000

**REASON FOR TOW**

___ A. WRECKED
___ B. ABANDONED
___ C. STOLEN
___ D. DRUG ARREST
___ E. TRAFFIC VIOLATION
___ F. OTHER (EXPLAIN BELOW)

| Signature & Badge # of Impounding Officer | Agency | Owner Notified ☐ Yes  ☐ No | DATE/TIME NOTIFIED |
|---|---|---|---|

| TO BE PREPARED BY WRECKER COMPANY AT SCENE PRIOR TO LEAVING SCENE | | | | |
|---|---|---|---|---|
| NAME OF PERSON TOWING | NAME OF TOW-IN COMPANY | | TELEPHONE NUMBER | |
| ADDRESS | CITY | | STATE | ZIP |
| TOW-IN FEE | DAILY STORAGE FEE | DATE STORED | TIME WRECKER CALLED | TIME ARRIVED |
| SIGNATURE OF PERSON TOWING | | | | |

## Document Vehicle Damage and Inventory:

## Damage

_____

_____

_____

## Inventory

_____

_____

_____

_____

| RELEASE INFORMATION - TO BE COMPLETED BY WRECKER COMPANY | |
|---|---|
| Met Conditions for vehicle Release<br>☐ Yes   ☐ No | ☐ Proof of Insurance<br>☐ Valid Registration<br>☐ Other _____ |
| Wrecker Information | Name of Wrecker:_____ Phone:_____<br><br>Name of authorized representative:_____<br><br>Signature: |
| Release Information | Released to:_____<br>          (Printed Name)         (Signature)<br><br>Form of ID presented:_____<br><br>Released by:_____<br>      Printed Name      Signature    Badge#<br><br>Date released:_____ Time released:_____ At scene ___Yes ___No |

# Vehicle Impound Incident Report

| Incident (non-criminal) | | | |
|---|---|---|---|
| Location | City | County | State |

| Title of Report: **ABANDONED VEHICLE - IMPOUND** | |
|---|---|
| Victim Name | Victim's Phone |
| Victim's Address | Victim's SSN |

| Date &Time of Tow | Date & Time Initially Reported to Dispatch | | | | | |
|---|---|---|---|---|---|---|
| Vehicle Involved?<br>☐ Yes ☐ No | VIN | Make | Model | Color | Year | License State |
| Name and address of Vehicle Owner | | | | | | |
| Name, address, and phone # of Wrecker that towed vehicle | | | | | | |

**NARRATIVE**

The above vehicle was found to be abandoned:

___ in violation of DOT regulations

___ (other): _____

**The vehicle was impounded by the above listed towing service on the date and time listed.**

The registered owner was determined by:

___ registration certificate or title in vehicle

___ computer check via Department of Motor Vehicle

___ all efforts failed to identify owner (explain in comments)

Owner notification of impound was made by: ___ Telephone   Date _____ Time _____

___ Certified mail   Date _____

___ All efforts of notification failed (explain in comments)

## Narrative of Report:

_____

_____

_____

_____

_____

_____

_____

_____

_____

_____

_____

_____

_____

_____

_____

| Officer's Name (printed) | Officer's Signature & Badge # | Date | Approved by Supervisor |
|---|---|---|---|
| | | | ☐ Yes      ☐ No |

# NOTICE OF VEHICLE CONFISCATION & REQUEST FOR CONFISCATION HEARING

## _____POLICE DEPARTMENT

As the owner of a _____ , (state) _____ license tag _____

VIN̆ _____ _____ you are hereby advised by that on

_____ the above referenced vehicle was confiscated by the

_____ Police Department upon the arrest of _____ .

The name of the confiscating agency is _____ .

     You may request a hearing before the Court and contest the confiscation of the attached referenced vehicle. Otherwise, the vehicle will proceed to forfeiture proceedings. To request a confiscation hearing, sign this document below and return to the Clerk of Court.

     Your request must be received by the Clerk within ten (10) days of your receipt of this notice. Otherwise, your right to the hearing is waived. If your request is timely received, the hearing will be held with ten (10) days of receipt of your request. You will be notified by First Class mail of the date, time and location of the hearing.

**I request a hearing.**

_____

Signature of Owner

_____

Address

_____                  _____

City              State         ZIP        Date of Request

# A E D
**A**utomatic **E**lectric **D**efibrillator   USE REPORT

_____ Department

| Case | Date of Incident: | Date of Report: |
|---|---|---|
| Officer Name & Badge | | |
| Location of Incident: | | |

**LOCATION TYPE:** □ Home    □ Public Place    □ Long Term Care Facility

□ Nursing Home    □ Other_____

## Patient Information

| Name: | | | |
|---|---|---|---|
| DOB: | | Age: | |
| State of ID | Type of ID | ID | |
| Home Address: | | | Phone: |
| Emergency Contact: | | | |
| Previous Medical History: | | | |

**CONDITION ON ARRIVAL:** □ Breathing with Pulse  □ Apneic with Pulse  □ Apneic No Pulse

Was Arrest Witnessed □ YES    □ NO        **ONSET OF COMPLAINT** _____:_____ (Time)

**COMPLAINT PRIOR TO COLLAPSE**_____

## Assistance Information

| Time Collapse: | | Time Bystander Started CPR: | |
|---|---|---|---|
| Bystander Name & Address: | | | |
| Time Called Received: | Time En route: | | Time Arrived at Scene: |
| Time Arrived at Patient's Side: | Time CPR Started: | | Time First Shock Delivered: |
| Time ACLS Arrived at Scene: | | ACLS Unit  : | |
| Time Initial Return of Pulse: | | | |

# CRIMINAL & JUVENILE REPORTS

# POLICE COMPLAINT - INFORMATION SUMMONS

| Court | Cause # (to be issued by court) |
|---|---|

☐ Complaint (Traffic)   ☐ Information (Criminal)   County of _____   City of _____

*I have probable cause to believe that on*

| Weekday | Day of Month | Month | Year | Time |
|---|---|---|---|---|
| Last Name | | First Name | | MI |
| Home Street Address | | | | |
| City | | | State | Zip Code |
| Race | Sex | Height | Weight | DOB | Age |

| ☐ DL  ☐ State ID  ☐ SSN  ☐ Other _____<br><br>Number: _____ | State | ☐ Commercial DL<br><br>☐ Operator's DL | CDL Class |
|---|---|---|---|

☐ Did unlawfully operate   ☐ Committed a violation as a passenger   in a vehicle described as

| Color | Vehicle Year | Make | License expiration year | License state | License plate # |
|---|---|---|---|---|---|

| ☐ Passenger Car/Pickup truck | ☐ Tractor  ☐ Tractor-trailer  ☐ Straight truck  ☐ Bus  ☐ Other |
|---|---|
| | ☐ DOT #  ☐ ICC # _____  ☐ Hazmat Placard # |

| At Location |
|---|

## DID COMMIT THE FOLLOWING VIOLATION

| Vehicle Speed | Speed Limit |
|---|---|
| Description of Offense: | |
| In Violation of Statute/Code: | |

*I affirm under penalty of perjury that the above information is true*

| Signature of Officer | Print Name | Police Dept. | Badge # |
|---|---|---|---|
| Court | Court Address & Phone # | Respond to Court By (date) | |
| Violator's Signature<br>COURT APPEARANCE PROMISE | *I promise to appear before the court when required. My signature is not an admission of guilt.* | **Approved by Solicitor/Prosecutor**<br><br>Signature: _____  Date: _____ | |

# MIRANDA WARNING

## _____POLICE DEPARTMENT_

Subject's Name: _____ SŠ_____ _____

Location of Interview: _____

Date: _____ Beginning Time of Interview_____ Ending Time of Interview_____

---

## *MIRANDA RIGHTS*

*Before we ask you any questions, you must understand your rights. Initial each line to indicate your understanding of, and agreement with, that line.*

_____ You have the right to remain silent.

_____ Anything you say can and will be used against you in a court of law.

_____ You have the right to talk to a lawyer for advice before we ask you any questions and to have him with you during questioning.

_____ If you cannot afford a lawyer, the court will appoint one to represent you without cost if you wish.

_____ If you decide to answer questions now without a lawyer present, you will still have the right to stop answering at any time. You also have the right to stop answering at any time until you talk to a lawyer.

_____ I have read this statement of my rights and I understand what my rights are.

## *WAIVER OF RIGHTS*

_____ I am willing to make a statement and answer questions. I do not want a lawyer at this time. I understand and know what I am doing. No promises or threats have been made to me and no pressure of any kind has been used against me.

_____  _____ Date: _____ Time: _____
     Print Name                 Signature

Witness: _____          _____
       Print Name                         Signature

Witness: _____          _____
       Print Name                         Signature

When interrogating juveniles, legal guardian signatures also required.

## *Legal Guardian of Juvenile*

As parent or legal guardian of_____, I have read the rights as set out above and understand them. Neither the juvenile nor I want a lawyer at this time and the juvenile is willing to answer questions.

Signed_____

Witness:_____

Witness:_____

Date_____ Time_____ ____.M.

# VOLUNTARY STATEMENT This is page _____ of ___.

_____ Police Department

Date_____ Place _____ time started _____

I, _____, am _____ years of age, being born on _____ have

been warned by _____, with the _____
police department, that I do not have to make any statement at all, nor answer any questions. I was also warned
and advised of my right to a lawyer of my own choice before or at any time during questioning, and if I am not
able to hire a lawyer, I may request to have a lawyer appointed to me. I do not now want a lawyer, and I waive
my right to the advice and presence of a lawyer, knowing that anything I say can and will be used against me in
a court of law. I now want to make a statement.

_____

_____

_____

_____

_____

_____

_____

_____

_____

_____

_____

_____

_____

*Draw a diagonal line through all unused space. Have person place initials at end of statement.*

**This form was completed at (time) _____.**

**Signature of person providing statement _____**

Witness_____ Signature_____ Badge _____
         Print name

Witness_____ Signature_____ Badge _____
         Print name

## *Interview Statement*

_____
_____
_____
_____
_____
_____
_____
_____
_____
_____
_____
_____
_____
_____
_____
_____
_____
_____
_____
_____
_____
_____
_____

*Draw a diagonal line through all unused space.  Have person place initials at end of statement.*

_____  _____  _____
    Print Name                 Signature              Date/Time

Witness_____  Signature_____
            Print name

Witness_____  Signature_____
            Print name

# CONSENT TO SEARCH

_____ Police Department

LOCATION_____

DATE_____ TIME_____ OFFICER_____

YOUR RIGHTS: YOU HAVE THE FOLLOWING CONSTITUTIONAL RIGHTS.

YOU HAVE THE RIGHT TO REQUIRE THAT A SEARCH WARRANT BE OBTAINED BEFORE ANY SEARCH OF YOUR PROPERTY & YOU HAVE THE RIGHT TO REFUSE TO CONSENT TO WARRANTLESS SEARCH.

YOU HAVE THE RIGHT TO TALK TO A LAWYER BEFORE GIVING CONSENT TO SUCH SEARCH.

IF YOU CANNOT AFFORD A LAWYER, ONE WILL BE APPOINTED TO YOU.

IF YOU ARE A JUVENILE, YOU HAVE THE RIGHT TO TALK WITH YOUR PARENT OR GUARDIAN BEFORE ANY CONSENT TO SUCH A SEARCH.

WAIVER AND CONSENT

BOTH WAIVERS AND CONSENTS MUST BE SIGNED IF JUVENILE.

**JUVENILE**: I HAVE READ THE STATEMENT OF MY RIGHTS AND I UNDERSTAND MY RIGHTS. I DO NOT WANT A LAWYER AT THIS TIME. I CONSENT TO A WARRANTLESS SEARCH BY OFFICERS OF THE POLICE DEPARTMENT OF THE FOLLOWING DESCRIBED PROPERTY LOCATED AT _____.
I AUTHORIZE THESE OFFICERS TO SEIZE ANY ARTICLE OF PROPERTY THAT THEY CONSIDER EVIDENCE. I UNDERSTAND AND KNOW WHAT I AM DOING. NO PROMISES OR THREATS HAVE BEEN MADE TO ME AND NO PRESSURE OR COERCION OF ANY KIND HAS BEEN USED AGAINST ME.

_____        _____        _____

Juvenile's Name (printed)                Juvenile's Name (signed)                Date

**LEGAL GUARDIAN**: AS PARENT OR LEGAL GUARDIAN OF (JUVENILE'S NAME) _____, I HAVE READ THE JUVENILE'S RIGHTS AND MY RIGHTS SET OUT ABOVE AND I UNDERSTAND THEM. NEITHER THE JUVENILE NOT I WANT A LAWYER AT THIS TIME. THE JUVENILE AND I CONSENT TO THE WARRANTLESS SEARCH OF OUR PROPERTY BY OFFICERS OF THE POLICE DEPARTMENT. I AUTHORIZE THE OFFICERS TO SEARCH THE FOLLOWING DESCRIBED PROPERTY LOCATED AT _____.

I FURTHER AUTHORIZE THEOFFICERS TO SEIZE ANY ARTICLE OF PROPERTY WHICH THEY CONSIDER EVIDENCE. I UNDERSTAND AND KNOW WHAT I AM DOING. NO PROMISES OR THREATS HAVE BEEN MADE TO ME AND NO PRESSURE OR COERCION OF ANY KIND HAS BEEN USED AGAINST ME.

_____        _____        _____

Legal Guardian's Name (printed)        Legal Guardian's Name (signed)        Date

WITNESSES (OFFICERS): _____        _____

Signed Name & Badge                Signed Name & Badge

130

# EXAMPLE 1: AFFIDAVIT FOR SEARCH WARRANT

State of <u>SC</u>

IN THE <u>SUPERIOR</u> COURT

County of <u>AIKEN</u>

CAUSE NO. _____


STATE OF <u>SC</u>

VS.

<u>**Blood of John Smith**</u>

<u>**w/m/DOB = 1/2/1987; SC DLN 568585**</u>

<u>**SNN 000-44-3432**</u>


COMES NOW, <u>Trp C. Allen (862)</u> (name of law enforcer), who being duly sworn upon oath, swears that he/she has good reason to believe that in the <u>body</u> described as <u>John Smith w/m/DOB = 1/2/1987; SC DLN 568585, SNN 000-44-3432</u> currently located at <u>Aiken City Police Dept.</u>, in Aiken County, <u>SC</u> (State) there is now in or about said <u>person</u>, being concealed certain property, namely: <u>blood that contains an illegal amount of alcohol for a driver in the state of SC</u>


Furthermore, the property:

_____ Was obtained unlawfully.

_____ Is possessed unlawfully.

_____ Is used or possessed with intent to be used as the means of committing another crime.

_____ XXX _____ Is concealed to prevent a crime from being discovered.

_____ XXX _____ Tends to show that a particular person committed a crime.

See record of proceedings for the facts and information tending to establish probable cause for the issuance of a search warrant.

This affidavit is made for the purpose of obtaining a search warrant from _____ Court, _____ County,

_____ (State) to examine _____ to search for the aforementioned evidence.


_____
(Affiant)

Subscribed and sworn to be true before me this _____ day of _____, 20____

_____        _____
Judge                                                              Court


131

# EXAMPLE 1: ORDER FOR SEARCH WARRANT

State of <u>SC</u>                              IN THE <u>SUPERIOR</u> COURT

County of <u>AIKEN</u>                         CAUSE NO. _____


STATE OF <u>SC</u>

VS.

<u>Blood of John Smith</u>

<u>w/m/DOB = 1/2/1987; SC DLN 568585</u>

<u>SNN 000-44-3432</u>


<u>Trp. C. Allen (862)</u> (name of law enforcer), is a sworn law enforcer and has presented testimony to establish

probable cause for the issuance of a search warrant. The court FINDS that the testimony presented does

describe the items to be searched, and the things to be searched for then seized;

That it sets forth that such are things to be searched for are concealed;

That it alleges substantially the offense in violation thereto;

That it sets forth that such search is for evidence that may be lawfully searched for and seized;

That probable cause does exist for the issuance of the requested search warrant and that a search warrant shall

be issued.


The officer who executes said search warrant shall make a return thereto directed to this court, which return

shall indicate the date and time searched and the list of items seized. Said items seized shall be securely held by

the law enforcement agency whose officer executed this warrant pursuant to Order of the court trying the cause.


SO ORDERED THIS _____ DAY OF _____ 20___.

JUDGE: _____

_____ COUNTY _____ COURT

# EXAMPLE 1: SEARCH WARRANT

State of  SC

County of AIKEN

IN THE  SUPERIOR  COURT

CAUSE NO. _____

STATE OF  SC

VS.

**Blood of John Smith**

**w/m/DOB = 1/2/1987; SC DLN 568585**

**SNN 000-44-3432**

To: Any Constable, Police Officer, Sheriff or Conservator of the Peace:

WHEREAS, there has presented before me testimony of  Trp. C. Allen (862) , a sworn law enforcement officer, for the purpose of establishing probable cause for the issuance of a Search Warrant. The Court, after hearing the testimony, now finds that probable cause exists for the issuance of said Search Warrant of the **location** described as follows:  body of John Smith,  w/m/DOB = 1/2/1981, SC DLN = 568585,  SNN 000-44-3432

YOU ARE, THEREFORE, commanded in the name of the State of  SC  with the necessary and proper assistance in the day time or night time to enter into the location aforementioned and there diligently search for **goods and chattels** described as blood that contains an illegal amount of alcohol for a driver in the state of SC

And that you are to bring the same or any part thereof found on such search forthwith before the Court and to be processed according to law.

GIVEN under my hand this _____ day of _____, 20____.

_____          _____ COUNTY _____ COURT
JUDGE

133

# EXAMPLE 2: AFFIDAVIT FOR SEARCH WARRANT

State of  SC                              IN THE  SUPERIOR  COURT

County of **AIKEN**                      CAUSE NO. _____

STATE OF  SC

VS.

**One 1995 Blue Ford Explorer**

**VIN 1F2HF72J858304372**

**SC Registration DV3842**

COMES NOW, Trp C. Allen (862)  (name of law enforcer), who being duly sworn upon oath, swears that he/she has good reason to believe that in the  vehicle  described as a  1995 Blue Ford Explorer, VIN 1F2HF72J858304372, SC Registration DV3842, currently located at 123 Elm Street, in Aiken County, SC  (State) there is now in or about  said vehicle, being concealed certain property, namely:

1. Packaged marijuana and paraphernalia.

Furthermore, the property:

_____XXX_____Was obtained unlawfully.

_____XXX_____Is possessed unlawfully.

_____XXX_____Is used or possessed with intent to be used as the means of committing another crime.

_____XXX_____Is concealed to prevent a crime from being discovered.

_____XXX_____Tends to show that a particular person  committed a crime.

See record of proceedings for the facts and information tending to establish probable cause for the issuance of a search warrant.

This affidavit is made for the purpose of obtaining a search warrant from  Aiken Superior  Court, Aiken County, SC  (State) to examine One 1995 Blue Ford Explorer, VIN 1F2HF72J858304372, SC Registration DV3842  to search for the aforementioned evidence.

_____          Subscribed and sworn to be true before me  this _____day of _____, 20____
(Affiant)

_____          _____
Judge                                    Court

# EXAMPLE 2: SEARCH WARRANT

**State of  SC**                                    IN THE  **SUPERIOR**  COURT

**County of AIKEN**                        CAUSE NO. _____


**STATE OF  SC**

**VS.**

**One 1995 Blue Ford Explorer**

**VIN 1F2HF72J858304372**

**SC Registration DV3842**


To: Any Constable, Police Officer, Sheriff or Conservator of the Peace:


WHEREAS, there has presented before me testimony of  Trp. C. Allen (862) , a sworn law enforcement officer, for the purpose of establishing probable cause for the issuance of a Search Warrant. The Court, after hearing the testimony, now finds that probable cause exists for the issuance of said Search Warrant of the **location** described as follows:  One 1995 Blue Ford Explorer, VIN 1F2HF72J858304372, SC Registration DV3842.


YOU ARE, THEREFORE, commanded in the name of the State of  SC  with the necessary and proper

assistance in the day time or night time to enter into the location aforementioned and there diligently search for

**goods and chattels** described as Marijuana, paraphernalia, and any other evidence of illegal drug trafficking.


And that you are to bring the same or any part thereof found on such search forthwith before the Court and to be processed

according to law.


GIVEN under my hand this _____ day of _____, 20____ .


_____          _____ COUNTY _____ COURT
            JUDGE


135

# AFFIDAVIT FOR SEARCH WARRANT

**State of** _____     **IN THE** _____ **COURT**

**County of** _____     **CAUSE NO.** _____

**STATE OF** _____

**VS.**

_____

_____

_____

COMES NOW, _____ (name of law enforcer), who being duly sworn upon oath, swears that

he/she has good reason to believe that in the _____ described as _____ ,

currently located at _____ , in _____ County, _____ (State) there is now in

or about said _____ , being concealed certain property, namely: _____

_____

Furthermore, the property:

_____ Was obtained unlawfully.

_____ Is possessed unlawfully.

_____ Is used or possessed with intent to be used as the means of committing another crime.

_____ Is concealed to prevent a crime from being discovered.

_____ Tends to show that a particular person committed a crime.

See record of proceedings for the facts and information tending to establish probable cause for the issuance of a search warrant.

This affidavit is made for the purpose of obtaining a search warrant from _____ Court, _____ County,

_____ (State) to examine _____ to search for the aforementioned evidence.

_____
(Affiant)

Subscribed and sworn to be true before me this _____ day of _____, 20____

_____     _____
Judge                           Court

# ORDER FOR SEARCH WARRANT

State of _____       IN THE _____ COURT

County of _____       CAUSE NO. _____


STATE OF _____

VS.

_____

_____

_____


_____ (name of law enforcer), is a sworn law enforcer and has presented testimony to

establish probable cause for the issuance of a search warrant. The court FINDS that the testimony presented

does describe the items to be searched, and the things to be searched for then seized;

That it sets forth that such are things to be searched for are concealed;

That it alleges substantially the offense in violation thereto;

That it sets forth that such search is for evidence that may be lawfully searched for and seized;

That probable cause does exist for the issuance of the requested search warrant and that a search warrant shall

be issued.


The officer who executes said search warrant shall make a return thereto directed to this court, which return

shall indicate the date and time searched and the list of items seized. Said items seized shall be securely held by

the law enforcement agency whose officer executed this warrant pursuant to Order of the court trying the cause.


SO ORDERED THIS _____ DAY OF _____ 20___.

JUDGE: _____

_____ COUNTY _____ COURT


137

# SEARCH WARRANT

State of _____          IN THE _____ COURT

County of _____          CAUSE NO. _____


STATE OF _____

VS.

_____

_____

_____


To: Any Constable, Police Officer, Sheriff or Conservator of the Peace:

WHEREAS, there has presented before me testimony of _____, a sworn law enforcement officer,

for the purpose of establishing probable cause for the issuance of a Search Warrant. The Court, after hearing the testimony,

now finds that probable cause exists for the issuance of said Search Warrant of the **location** described as follows: _____

_____


YOU ARE, THEREFORE, commanded in the name of the State of _____ with the necessary and proper assistance

in the day time or night time to enter into the location aforementioned and there diligently search for **goods and chattels**

described as

_____

_____


And that you are to bring the same or any part thereof found on such search forthwith before the Court and to be processed

according to law.


GIVEN under my hand this _____ day of _____, 20____.


_____          _____ COUNTY _____ COURT
                JUDGE

# Field Interview Card

_____ Police Department

| County | Date | Time |
|---|---|---|
| Department Incident Number | Reason for contact | |

| Location of Contact | Pedestrian Stop <br><br> ☐ Y ☐ N | Traffic Stop ☐ Y ☐ N <br><br> ☐ Driver ☐ Passenger |
|---|---|---|
| Disposition | | |

| Name of Subject | Nickname |
|---|---|
| Address | Phone |

| State ID or Driver's License | | State | SSN | | | |
|---|---|---|---|---|---|---|

| Age | Sex | Race | Height | Weight | Build | Complexion |
|---|---|---|---|---|---|---|
| DOB | POB | Hair | Eyes | Marks/Tattoos (Type & Location) | | |

| Subject's Parents' Names |
|---|
| Clothing Description |
| Persons with Subject at Scene |
| Gang Affiliation |

| Vehicle Make | Model | VIN |
|---|---|---|
| Color | Tag | State |
| Owner of Vehicle | | Owner at Scene ☐ Y ☐ N |

# POLICE DEPARTMENT - INTELLIGENCE REPORT

DATE:_____ TIME:_____ OFFICER & BADGE :_____

SUBJECT NAME:_____ ALIAS:_____

DOB:_____ AGE:_____ RACE:_____ SEX:_____

SSN:_____ DL _____ STATE:_____

HEIGHT:_____ WEIGHT:_____ HAIR:_____ EYES:_____

SCARS, MARKS, TATTOOS:_____

OCCUPATION:_____

ADDRESS:_____ PHONE:_____

VEHICLE DESCRIPTION:_____

SUBJECT'S ASSOCIATES:_____

STATUS OF SUBJECT (CIRCLE ONE)　　**SUSPECT　　WANTED　　ARRESTED**

INFORMATION SOURCE:_____

NOTES (Articulate reason for suspicion):_____

_____

_____

_____

_____

_____

_____

_____

# SUSPECT REPORT

## POLICE DEPARTMENT

Case _____          PAGE___OF____

<table>
<tr><td rowspan="4">CRIME</td><td colspan="2">CRIME TITLE</td><td>CODE</td><td>LOCATION</td><td>DATE</td></tr>
</table>

| | | | | |
|---|---|---|---|---|
| **CRIME** | CRIME TITLE | CODE | LOCATION | DATE |

| **SUSP. VEH** | LICENSE | STATE | YEAR | MAKE | MODEL | BODY STYLE __2DR __4DR __CONVERT __P/U __ STRAIGHT TRUCK __VAN ___RV ___M/C ___OTHER |
|---|---|---|---|---|---|---|

| COLOR/COLOR | OTHER CHARACTERISTICS | DISPOSTION OF VEHICLE |
|---|---|---|

REGISTERED OWNER

| **SUSPECT** | SUSPECT NAME | SEX | RACE: __UK __HISP __NATIVE AM. __ASIAN __WHT __BLK __OTH |
|---|---|---|---|

| AKA | DOB | AGE | HT | WT | BUILD: __THIN __MEDIUM __UK __HEAVY __MUSCLR |
|---|---|---|---|---|---|

| HAIR: __BLK __BRN __RED __BLN __GRAY __WHITE __N/A __OTHER __UK | EYES: __BLK __GRN __GRAY __UK __BRN __BLU __HAZEL __OTHER |
|---|---|

| RESIDENCE ADDRESS | STATE | ZIP | RES. PHONE | SSN |
|---|---|---|---|---|
| BUSINESS ADDRESS | STATE | ZIP | BUS PHONE | OCCUPATION |

| CLOTHING | ARRESTED ☐YES ☐NO | STATUS ☐DRIVER ☐PED ☐PASS | GANG AFFILIATION: HOW KNOWN: |
|---|---|---|---|

DL STATE &

| AMOUNT OF HAIR | HAIR STYLE | COMPLEXION | TATTOOS/SCARS | WEAPON(S) |
|---|---|---|---|---|
| __UNKNOWN<br>__THICK<br>__THIN<br>__RECEDING<br>__BALD<br>__OTHER | __UNKNOWN<br>__LONG<br>__SHORT<br>__COLLAR<br>__MILITARY<br>__CREW CUT<br>__RIGHT PART<br>__LEFT PART<br>__CENTER PART<br>__STRAIGHT<br>__PONY TAIL<br>__AFRO<br>__TEASED<br>__OTHER | __UNKNOWN<br>__CLEAR<br>__ACNE<br>__POCKED<br>__FRECKLED<br>__WEATHERED<br>__ALBINO<br>__OTHER | __UNKNOWN<br>__FACE<br>__TEETH<br>__NECK<br>__R/ARM<br>__L/ARM<br>__R/HAND<br>__L/HAND<br>__R/LEG<br>__L/LEG<br>__R/SHOULDER<br>__L/SHOULDER<br>__FRONT TORSO<br>__BACK TORSO<br>__OTHER | __UNKNOWN<br>__CLUB<br>__HANDGUN<br>__OTHER UNK GUN<br>__RIFLE<br>__SHOTGUN<br>__TOYGUN<br>__SIMULATED<br>__POCKET KNIFE<br>__BUTCHER KNIFE<br>__HANDS/FEET<br>__BODILY FORCE<br>__STRNGULATION<br>__TIRE IRON<br>__OTHER |

| TYPE OF HAIR | FACIAL HAIR | GLASSES | UNIQUE CLOTHING | HAD WEAPON IN OR ABOUT |
|---|---|---|---|---|
| __UNKNOWN<br>__CLEAN<br>__DIRTY<br>__GREASY<br>__MATTED<br>__ODOR<br>__OTHER | __UNKNOWN<br>__N/A<br>__CLN SHAVEN<br>__MOUSTACHE<br>__FULL BEARD<br>__GOATEE<br>__FU MANCHU<br>__LOWER LIP<br>__SIDE BURNS<br>__FUZZ<br>__UNSHAVEN<br>__OTHER | __UNKNOWN<br>__NONE<br>__YES<br>__REG GLASSES<br>__SUN GLASSES<br>__WIRE FRAME<br>__PLASTIC FRAME<br>__COLOR<br>__OTHER | __UNKNOWN<br>__NONE<br>__CAP/HAT<br>__GLOVES<br>__SKI MASK<br>__STOCKING MASK<br>__OTHER | __UNKNOWN<br>__N/A<br>__BAG/BRIEFCASE<br>__NEWSPAPER<br>__POCKET<br>__SHOULDER<br>__HOLSTER<br>__WAISTBAND<br>__OTHER |

| R/L HANDED | VOICE | WEAPON FEATURE |
|---|---|---|
| __UNKOWN<br><br>__RIGHT<br><br>__LEFT | __UNKNOWN<br>__N/A<br>__LISP<br>__SLURRED<br>__STUTTER<br>__ACCENT<br>__DESCRIBE_____<br>__OTHER | __UNKNOWN<br>__ALTERED STOCK<br>__SAWED OFF<br>__AUTOMATIC<br>__BOLT ACTION<br>__PUMP<br>__REVOLVER<br>__BLUE STEEL<br>__CHROME/NICKEL<br>__DOUBLE BARREL<br>__SINGLE BARREL<br>__OTHER |
| Officer's Name (printed) | Officer's Signature & Badge # | Date | Approved by Supervisor<br><br>□ Yes  □ No |

# Case Report Checklist Attachments

**INSTRUCTIONS: Complete this cover. Place case number on <u>each</u> attachment.**


Case _____

Vehicle Impound _____ Property Record & Receipt _____


_____ Arrest Report

_____ Advice of Rights/Consent to Search

_____ PC Affidavits/General Operating While Intoxicated

_____ Charging Information

_____ Hit Confirmation

_____ Court Orders

_____ Coroner's Report

_____ Crash Report

_____ Request for Lab Exam

_____ Certificate of Analysis

_____ Technician's Report

_____ Warrant

_____ Witness Statements

_____ Other: _____


**Number of pages, including this page (required):** _____

# INVESTIGATIVE CHECKLIST

Case Number_____

Case Report Complete?    ☐Y    ☐N

Comments

1. Crime Scene Visited?   Y__ N__    _____

2. V's Statement Obtained Y__ N__    _____

3. W's Statement Obtained Y__ N__    _____

4. Suspect's Statement Obtained Y__ N__    _____

5. Suspect Arrested Y__ N__    _____

6. Crime Scene Searched Y__ N__    _____

7. Physical Evidence Obtained Y__ N__    _____

8. Usable Prints Obtained Y__ N__    _____

9. Photos Taken at Scene Y__ N__    _____

10. Serial Numbers Obtained Y__ N__    _____

11. Vehicle Used Y__ N__    _____

12. Positive Canvas Results Y__ N__    _____

13. Familiar M.O. Pattern Y__ N__    _____

14. Complainant Willing to Press Charges Y__ N__    _____

15. Vict and/or Wit Shown Mug Shots Y__ N__    _____

16. Photo Line-Up Conducted Y__ N__    _____

17. Field Contact Info. Reviewed Y__ N__    _____

18. Evidence Sent to Lab Y__ N__    _____

19. Officers on Scene Interviewed Y__ N__    _____

20. Positive Info from Informants Y__ N__    _____

21. Copies of Officers' Supplements Received Y__ N__    _____

22. Lab Reports Received Y__ N__    _____

23. Conference w/Pros. Attorney Y__ N__    _____

# LEAD SHEET

Case Number:_____  Date:_____

Time:_____

Information Received Via:

□Telephone          □ In Person          □ Written Communication

□ Other

(Specify)_____

Information Received From:

Name:_____  Address:_____

Telephone Number: Home_____  Work_____  Cell_____

Information Received:

_____

_____

_____

_____

_____

Action Taken:

_____

_____

_____

_____

_____

Name of Lead Officer:_____

# Case Report (criminal)

| Case (criminal) ˇ | | | |
|---|---|---|---|
| Location of Offense | City | County | State |
| Offense | | Code | |
| Victim Name | | Victim's Phone | |
| Victim's Address | | Victim's SSN | |

| Victim's Sex | Victim's Race | Indication of Hate Crime<br>☐ Yes ☐ No | Victim Injured<br>☐ Yes ☐ No | Name of Facility that Treated Victim |
|---|---|---|---|---|

| Address of Facility that Treated Victim |
|---|

| Date &Time of Offense | Date &Time Reported to Dispatch | Dispatch Badge # |
|---|---|---|

| Person Who Reported Crime (include name & address) |
|---|

| Witness to Crime (name and address) |
|---|

| Suspect (name & address) | DOB | SSN |
|---|---|---|

| Description(Sex/Race/Ht/Wt/Hair/Eyes/Scars/Tattoos/Clothing) |
|---|

| Arrested? | MUG # | Citation # | Property Form # |
|---|---|---|---|

| Weapon, Tool, or Force |
|---|

| Vehicle Involved?<br>☐ Yes ☐ No | VIN | Make | Model | Color | Year | License State |
|---|---|---|---|---|---|---|

| Name and address of Vehicle Owner |
|---|

| Name, address, and phone # of Wrecker that towed vehicle |
|---|

**NARRATIVE** (First indicate MOTIVE & MO.  Then list additional Suspects, Victims, Witnesses, Vehicles, etc.)

ATTACHMENTS:

| Officer's Name (printed) | Officer's Signature & Badge # | Date | Approved by Supervisor |
|---|---|---|---|
| | | | ☐ Yes   ☐ No |

# Supplemental Case Report

| Case (criminal) | | | |
|---|---|---|---|
| Location of Offense | City | County | State |
| Offense | | | Code |
| Victim Name | | Victim's Phone | |
| Summary: | | | |
| | | | |
| | | | |
| | | | |
| | | | |
| | | | |
| | | | |
| | | | |
| | | | |
| | | | |
| | | | |
| | | | |
| ATTACHMENTS: | | | |

| Officer's Name (printed) | Officer's Signature & Badge # | Date | Approved by Supervisor □ Yes □ No |
|---|---|---|---|
| | | | |

# FINAL DISPOSITION OF CASE

_____ Police Department

| Case (criminal) | | Page | of | Date |
|---|---|---|---|---|
| Title of Offense | | Code | | |
| Victim's Name | | Victim's Phone | | |
| Victim's Address | | | | |
| Name of Defendant: | | | | |
| Original Charge: | | | | |
| Final Charge: | | | | |
| Date of Trial:          Court:          Cause | | | | |

◊ Dismissed     ◊ Acquitted     ◊ Nolle Prosecuted     ◊ Guilty

Fine: $          Court Cost: $

Sentence (check one): ◊ Committed   ◊ Suspended   Defendant Appealed?   ◊ Yes   ◊ No

Disposition of Evidence Collected (need judge order as attachment):

Attachments:

| Officer's Name (printed) | Officer's Signature & Badge # | Date | Approved by Supervisor |
|---|---|---|---|
| | | | ☐ Yes   ☐ No |

# AFFIDAVIT FOR PROBABLE CAUSE (General)

State of _____          IN THE _____ COURT

County of _____          CAUSE NO. _____


**STATE OF** _____

**VS.**

_____

**DOB:** _____

**SSN:** _____


**FOR OFFENSE (title):**_____ **Code:** _____


COMES NOW, _____, who being duly sworn upon oath, says that:

1. He/She is an officer with the _____ Department, and believes the following to be

   true.

2. On or about: (date of offense) _____ 20___, at the following location: _____

   _____, which is in _____ County, _____ (State),

   one (defendant) _____

3. Did then and there commit the following violation (code) _____, by

   (describe the specific act that supports the criminal charge via **elements of the crime**) _____

   _____

   _____

   _____

_____

_____

_____

_____

4.   This officer believes the above facts to be true because (check all that apply)

☐ I personally observed the activity described herein.

☐ The above was told to me by another sworn law enforcement officer, upon whom I have relied on in the past for information and found his/her information to be credible without exception.

☐ The above was told to me by the victim of a crime, who has no apparent motive to lie, and said statement was given in a straightforward and non-evasive manner, which indicated that the statement was credible.

☐ The above was told to me by a witness of a crime, who has no apparent motive to lie, and said statement was given in a straightforward and non-evasive manner, which indicated that the statement was credible. Further, witness' statement was corroborated by independent evidence.

☐ The above was told to me by the defendant, which was a statement made against his/her penal interests. Further, Defendant's statement was corroborated by independent evidence.

**I swear or affirm under penalty of perjury that the foregoing representations are true.**

Dated on this _____ day of _____, 20_____

_____
Arresting Officer's Name & Badge #

Approved by: _____
Prosecutor

151

# INFORMATION FOR VIOLATION OF LAW

State of _____          IN THE _____ COURT

County of _____          CAUSE NO. _____


STATE OF _____

VS.

_____

**DOB:** _____

**SSN:** _____


**INFORMATION FOR (OFFENSE TITLE):** _____

**CODE** _____          **CLASS** _____          ☐ **MISDEMEANOR**          ☐ **FELONY**


COMES NOW, _____ (name of officer), who being duly sworn upon oath,

says that on or about : (date of offense) _____, 20___, at (location of offense) _____

_____, in _____ County, _____ (State), one

(defendant) _____ of (Defendant's address) _____

_____ did then and there RECKLESSLY, KNOWINGLY, or

INTENTIONALLY: (describe **elements of the crime**)

_____

_____

_____

_____

_____

_____

_____

_____

_____

_____

_____

_____

All of which is contrary to the form of the statute in such cases made and provided, and against the peace and dignity of the State of _____.

**I swear or affirm under penalty of perjury that the foregoing representations are true.**

Dated on this _____ day of _____, 20____

_____

ARRESTING OFFICER'S NAME & BADGE

Witness List:

Approved by: _____

PROSECUTOR

# APPLICATION FOR CRIMINAL ARREST WARANT

_____ Police Department     Case _____

**Defendant's name** _____ AKA _____

Address _____

Phone _____

SSN _____ State of ID _____ Type of ID _____ ID __ _____

DOB _____ Age _____

Description (race/sex/ht/wt/tattoos/scars) _____


**Prosecuting Information:** Police Department _____ ORI _____

Affiant's name (Officer) _____ Badge _____ _

Affiant's Address _____


**Nature of Offense** Title of Criminal Offense _____ Code _____

Incident Date _____ Incident Time _____

Incident Location _____

Victim Name _____ Address _____ Phone _____

Witness Name _____ Address _____ Phone _____

Witness/Victim statements attached   □ Yes    □ No


**Elements of offense** _____

_____

_____

_____

**Affiant's Name** _____ Signature _____ Date _____

**Approved by Judge** (name) _____ Signature _____ Date _____

# ARREST WARRANT

☐ County   ☐ City    of State: _____

STATE OF _____

   VS.

_____ (name of defendant)

Defendant's Address _____

Phone _____ SSN _____

Sex ___ Race ___ Height ___ Weight ___ DL State ___ DL _____ _____

Prosecuting Police Agency _____

Prosecuting Police Officer _____

Offense Title _____ Offense Code _____

This warrant is CERTIFIED FOR SERVICE in the    ☐ County  ☐ City  of _____

**The accused is to be brought before this court according to law.**

Judge's signature _____ Court _____ Date _____

**EXECUTION OF WARRANT**

A copy of this arrest warrant was delivered to the defendant on _____ (date).

Law Enforcer _____ Signature _____

Badge _____ Department _____

**RETURN ARREST WARRANT TO:**

_____ (Court & Address)

# ARREST WARRANT

State of _____

Personally appeared before this court, the affiant _____

being duly sworn deposes and says that the defendant _____

did within this county and state on or about _____ (date) violate the criminal

laws of the state of _____ (or ordinance of ☐ County ☐ City of _____ ).  The

defendant violated  the following law: Title of Offense _____ ,

Code _____.  I further state that there is probable cause to believe that the

defendant named above did commit the crime set forth and that probable cause is based on

the following facts: (must state **elements of the crime**)

_____

_____

_____

_____

_____

_____

_____

_____

_____



Affiant's Name (printed) _____ Badge _____

Signature of Affiant _____ Department's Phone _____

Department's Address _____

**ARREST WARRANT** - TO ANY LAW ENFORER OF THIS STATE:

It appearing from the above affidavit that there are reasonable grounds to believe that on or

about _____ (date) the defendant _____

did violate the criminal laws of the State of _____ (or ordinance of ☐ County ☐ City of

_____ ) as set forth: Title of offense _____

Code _____

Having found probable cause, you are empowered to arrest the defendant and to bring the

defendant before this court. A copy of the ARREST WARRANT shall be delivered to the

defendant at the time of execution or as soon thereafter as practical.

Signature of Judge _____ Court _____ Date _____

# ARREST WARRANT SERVICE REPORT

_____ Police Department

Case _____ Date _____

Agency ORI _____

Defendant _____

Arrest Date _____ (date of warrant execution)

Arrest Time _____

Arrest Location _____


Warrant _____ _____

Issue Date _____

Title of Offense _____ Code _____

Offense Date _____

Affiant _____ Badge _____ _____ Dept. _____

Victim _____


Was defendant taken to Judge at time of arrest?    □ Yes   □ No

Was defendant released on bond?        □ Yes   □ No

Defendant is      □ adult    □ juvenile

# Example of MUG Sheet

(used when photographing suspect at jail during booking process)

# DOE, JOHN L.

# DOB = 10-17-1936

# Mug # AA-1224

# WAYNE POLICE DEPARTMENT

# DATE = 02-07-2014

# CONSULAR NOTIFICATION

### FAX SHEET FOR NOTIFYING CONSULAR OFFICERS OF ARREST OR DETENTION

_____POLICE DEPARTMENT     DATE: _____ TIME: _____

TO: EMBASSY /CONSULATE OF _____ in _____, _____

                                (COUNTRY)               (CITY)           (STATE)

SUBJECT: NOTIFICATION OF ARREST/DETENTION OF A NATIONAL FROM YOUR COUNTRY

FROM: _____ (INVESTIGATING OFFICER'S NAME)

_____POLICE DEPARTMENT

_____ (address)

Phone: _____      FAX: _____

WE ARRESTED/DETAINED THE FOLLOWING FOREIGN NATIONAL, WHOM WE UNDERSTAND TO BE A NATIONAL OF YOUR COUNTRY, ON _____ (date)

MR./MRS./MS:_____

DOB: _____

PLACE OF BIRTH: _____

PASSPORT NUMBER: _____

DATE OF PASSPORT ISSUANCE: _____

PLACE OF PASSPORT ISSUANCE_____

TO ARRANGE FOR CONSULAR ACCESS, PLEASE CALL _____

WHEN YOU CALL, PLEASE REFER TO DEPARTMENT'S CASE NUMBER: _____

COMMENTS:_____

_____

_____

_____

_____

# CONSULAR NOTIFICATION

## _____ Police Department

WHEN A FOREIGN NATIONAL IS ARRESTED OR DETAINED, THE ARRESTING/INVESTIGATING OFFICER SHALL DETERMINE, TO THE BEST OF HIS/HER ABILITY, THE FOREIGN NATIONAL'S COUNTRY.

FOREIGN NATIONAL'S COUNTRY:_____

COUNTRY REQUIRING MANDATORY NOTIFICATION?    ☐ YES    ☐ NO

\*\*\*\*\*\*\*\*\*\*\*\*\*\*\*\*\*\*\*\*\*\*\*\*\*\*\*\*\*\*\*\*\*\*\*\*\*\*\*\*\*\*\*\*\*\*\*\*\*\*\*\*\*\*\*\*\*\*\*\*\*\*\*\*\*\*\*\*\*\*\*\*\*\*\*\*\*\*\*\*\*\*\*\*

UTILIZE THIS SECTION WHEN MANDATORY NOTIFICATION IS NOT REQUIRED.

IT IS NOT REQUIRED THAT WE NOTIFY YOUR COUNTRY'S CONSULAR REPRESENTATIVES HERE IN THE UNITED STATES THAT YOU HAVE BEEN ARRESTED OR DETAINED. HOWEVER, IF YOU LIKE, YOU CAN REQUEST US TO MAKE NOTIFICATION NOW, OR AT ANY TIME IN THE FUTURE.

DO YOU WANT US TO NOTIFY YOUR COUNTRY'S CONSULAR OFFICIALS?  ☐ YES    ☐ NO

\*\*\*\*\*\*\*\*\*\*\*\*\*\*\*\*\*\*\*\*\*\*\*\*\*\*\*\*\*\*\*\*\*\*\*\*\*\*\*\*\*\*\*\*\*\*\*\*\*\*\*\*\*\*\*\*\*\*\*\*\*\*\*\*\*\*\*\*\*\*\*\*\*\*\*\*\*\*\*\*\*\*\*\*

FOREIGN NATIONAL'S PRINTED NAME: _____

FOREIGN NATIONAL'S SIGNED NAME: _____

WITNESS PRINTED NAME: _____

WITNESS SIGNED NAME: _____

DATE: _____

# Jail Intake Form

## _____ Police Department Booking Record

| Booking Number | Arresting Agency | ORI | State ID | MUG | Inmate's Photograph |
|---|---|---|---|---|---|
| Name | Sex | Race | Height | Weight | |
| Date of Birth | Hair | Complexion | Build | Eyes | |
| SSN | Home Phone | Work Phone | Marital Status | Resident Status | |
| Driver's License | State of DL | Home Address | | Place of Birth | |

**Information Given at time of Booking**      DOB      SSN            Address
Name:

| Gang Affiliation | Tattoos | Place & Address of Employment |
|---|---|---|

**Emergency Contact Information**
Name:                          Address:                          Home phone  :

| Ill or Injured  __YES  __NO | TYPE OF ILLNESS OF INJURY | Type of Medication Taking |
|---|---|---|

Special Management for Inmate  __Medical  __Mental  __Suicidal  __High Security  __Other (Describe):

| Arresting Officer | Arrest Date/Time | Arrest Location | |
|---|---|---|---|
| Booking Officer | Booking Date/Time | Booking Status (Complete/Pending) | |
| Received by Officer | Custodial Search by | | |
| Charge 1 (Title) | State Code | Charge Level (M or F) & Class (A-F) | |
| Charge 2 (Title) | State Code | Charge Level (M or F) & Class (A-F) | |
| Charge 3 (Title) | State Code | Charge Level (M or F) & Class (A-F) | |
| Arresting Officer's Signature | Arresting Officer's Badge | Arresting Officer's Department | |
| Fine | Bail | Disposition | |
| **Inmate Tracking #** | Intake Date | Block | Cell |
| Scheduled Release Date | Actual Release Date | Release Type | |

# CUSTODY ORDER / CUSTODY HOLD

**Name of Jailer Accepting Inmate:** _____ **Signature:** _____


**Inmate's Name:** _____ **Today's Date:** _____

**Inmate's DOB:** _____ **Inmate's SSN:** _____

**Inmate's ID#:** _____ **Type of ID:** _____


**Court Assigned to Case:** _____

**Court Date (Appearance Date/Time):** _____


**Charge #1 (title and code):** _____

Level _____ Class _____

**Charge #2 (title and code):** _____

Level _____ Class _____

**Charge #3 (title and code):** _____

Level _____ Class _____

**Charge #4 (title and code):** _____

Level _____ Class _____


**Arresting Officer's Name (print):** _____

**Signature:** _____

**Badge #:** _____ **Department:** _____

# TEMPORARY HOLD FORM - DETENTION DIVISION

## _____POLICE DEPARTMENT

THE FOLLOWING ARRESTEE:_____

DOB:_____    SŠ _____

CHARGED WITH THE CRIME(S) OF:_____

HAS BEEN PLACED INTO THE CUSTODY OF THE DETENTION CENTER BY

OFFICER (NAME & BADGĚ ): _____
PLEASE PRINT NAME

AS AN AGENT FOR: _____
POLICE AGENCY

TO BE HELD UNTIL THE NEXT SCHEDULED BOND HEARING, OR A MAXIMUM OF 24 HOURS. THE LAW ENFORCEMENT OFFICER NAMED IN THIS ORDER WILL APPEAR AT THE APPROPRIATE COURT FOR THE PURPOSE OF OBTAINING WARRANT(S) FOR THE ABOVE STATED CHARGES.

THIS FORM MAY NOT BE USED FOR TICKABLE OFFENSE

REASON FOR A TEMPORARY HOLD:

_____ NO MAGISTRATE IS AVAILABLE AT TIME OF CUSTODY EXCHANGE.

_____ THE ARRESTEE IS TOO COMBATIVE TO APPEAR BEFORE A MAGISTRATE AT THIS TIME.

_____THE ARRESTEE IS IMPAIRED DUE TO DRUGS/ALCOHOL.

_____ THE POLICE AGENCY IS EXPERIENCING AN UNUSUALLY HIGH BACK-LOG OF CALLS.


AUTHORIZING LAW ENFORMENT OFFICER:          RECEIVING DETENTION OFFICER:




_____          _____
SIGNATURE     BADGĚ     DATE/TIME          SIGNATURE     BADGĚ     DATE/TIME

# Fingerprint Card Information

Criminal = Red

Applicant = Blue

Juvenile = Yellow

**BELOW IS GENERAL INFORMATION THAT IS REQUIRED ON FINGERPRINT CARDS. THE INFORMATION IS GATHERED AT THE TIME OF BOOKING AT THE JAIL.**

Police Dept ORI _____ Name of Police Dept _____

Police address _____

Date of arrest _____ Date of offense _____

Suspect's place of birth (State) _____ Country of Citizen _____

Suspect's Name _____ AKA _____

Residence _____

SSN _____ Sex ___ Race ___ Height ___ Weight ___ Hair ___ Eyes ___

Tattoos, marks, scars _____ Photo Available ___ Yes ___ No

FBI _____ _____ State Criminal ID _____

Local ID ( MUG ) __ _____

Signature of suspect _____

Name of officer who fingerprinted suspect _____

Suspect's Employers _____

Suspect's Occupation _____

Charge _____ Code _____

Father _____ Address _____

Mother _____ Address _____

Spouse _____ Address _____

Reason for Caution _____

Person to be notified in case of emergency _____

# Example - Latent Print Card

Date: <u>01-07-2014</u>

Case # <u>2014-1107-2304</u>

Lift # <u>5</u>

Type of Offense: <u>Kidnapping</u>

Victim: <u>Jane Doe</u>

Address Location from which prints were obtained: <u>38348 Alberta St</u>
<u>Aiken, SC 29801 Parking Lot 6</u>

Prints Lifted From (Object) <u>Compact Disk</u>

Prints Lifted By <u>Trp. Chris Rachwal</u>      Badge # <u>717</u>

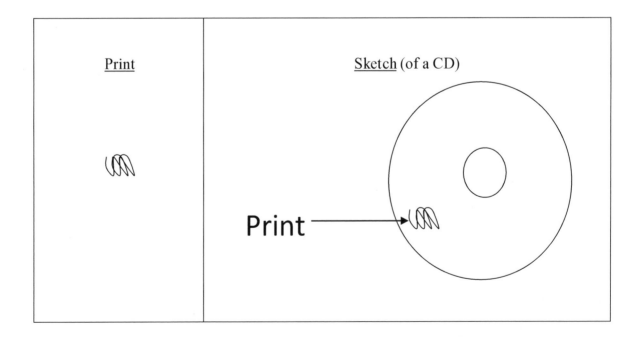

# Latent Print Card

Date: _____

Case # _____

Lift # _____

Type of Offense: _____

Victim: _____

Address Location from which prints were obtained: _____

_____

Prints Lifted From (Object) _____

Prints Lifted By _____ Badge # _____

| Print | Sketch |
|-------|--------|
|       |        |
|       |        |
|       |        |
|       |        |
|       |        |

# PROBABLE CAUSE DECLARATION - BAIL SETTING INFORMATION

_____POLICE DEPARTMENT          BOOKING NO. _____

| DEFENDANT (LAST, FIRST, MIDDLE) | | DOB |
|---|---|---|
| ADDRESS (RESIDENCE) | | |
| BOOKING CHARGE(S) | CODE(S) | HOLDS |
| DATE/TIME OF ARREST | | 48 HR. EXP DATE/TIME |
| ARRESTING AGENCY | | ARRESTING OFFICER & BADGE |

**FACTS ESTABLISHING ELEMENTS OF CRIME(S):**

_____

_____

_____

_____

_____

☐ SEE ATTACHED REPORTS

☐ VICTIM'S AGE: _____ VICTIM'S INJURIES_____

☐ WEAPON DESCRIPTION_____

☐ VALUE OF PROPERTY LOSS_____ TYPE OF PROPERTY _____

☐ TYPE OF ILLEGAL DRUGS_____ QTY_____

☐ WHOLESALE VALUE_____ STREET VALUE_____

I DECLARE UNDER PENALTY OF PERJURY THAT THE FOREGOING INFORMATION IS TRUE AND
ACCURATE.

_____
OFFICER NAME          SIGNATURE          BADGE          DATE/TIME

# NARCOTICS OR INTOXICATION REPORT

_____ Police Department     Case # _____

| Offense | Location of Occurrence | County |
|---|---|---|

| Name | AKA |
|---|---|

| Address | DOB | Place of Birth |
|---|---|---|

| Sex    Race   Age   Height    Weight    Hair    Eyes | Occupation |
|---|---|

| Any Recent Illnesses? When? | What | On prescription medicine?  ☐ Yes   ☐ No | Name of current prescription medications? |
|---|---|---|---|

**Advisement of Rights**

You have the right to remain silent

Anything you say may be used against you in court

You have the right to an attorney before and during questioning

If you cannot afford an attorney, one will be appointed for you before questioning if you wish (Do you understand?)

I NOW WISH TO TALK WITHOUT A LAWYER _____ Individual's Signature

Examination Location

Method of Consumption

What?   Circle all that apply.     Name of drug _____

Depressant  Inhalant  Phencyclidine  Cannabis  Stimulate  Hallucinogen  Narcotic

Physical Consequences:   Nystagmus: ☐ Yes ☐ No     Pupils: ☐ Dilated ☐ Constricted

Pulse Blood Pressure _____   Body Temperature _____   Obsessive Scratching ☐ Yes ☐ No

| Officer's Name (printed) | Officer's Signature & Badge | Date | Approved by Supervisor  ☐ Yes   ☐ No |
|---|---|---|---|

# CORRECTIONAL MEDICAL SURVEY

INTAKE SCREENING AND TRIAGE

Date Booked In _____ NAME _____ BOOKING ___ _____ DOB _____ SEX ___

| **STATEMENT OF BOOKING OFFICER** |
| --- |
| DOES THE INMATE SEEM TO BE UNDER THE INFLUENCE OF DRUGS, IMPAIRED, OR INJURED IN ANY WAY? ___YES___NO Comments _____ |
| OFFICER'S SIGNATURE:                    DEPT:                         DATE: |

MEDICAL/MENTAL QUESTIONNAIRE

1. DO YOU HAVE ANY OF THE FOLLOWING PROBLEMS?

| | | | |
| --- | --- | --- | --- |
| __ASTHMA | __ENT PROBLEMS | __HERNIA | __INTESTINAL DISORDERS |
| __BACK INJURIES | __FX/SPRAINS | __HIV/AIDS | __MENATL PROBLEMS |
| __DEFORMITIES | __HEART TROUBLE | __HIGH BLOOD PRESSURE | __PSYCH. HOSPITAL |
| __TUBERCULOSIS | __DENTAL PROBLEMS | __STD | __HEPATITIS: TYPE____ |
| __DIABETES | __SEIZURES | __PREGNANT/DUE DATE:_____ | |

__OTHER_____ ALLERGIES_____

| | Y | N |
| --- | --- | --- |
| 2. ARE YOU TAKING OR DO YOU NEED TO TAKE ANY PRESCRIBED MEDICATIONS (INCLUDING PSYCHIATRIC, BIRTH CONTROL PILLS)? | | |
| 3. HAVE YOU EVER BEEN TREATED FOR TUBERCULOSIS? | | |
| 4. HAVE YOU HAD A COUGH FOR MORE THAN THREE WEEKS WITH ANY OF THE FOLLOWING: FEVER, WEIGHT LOSS, FATIGUE, NIGHT SWEATS? | | |
| 5. HAVE YOU HAD A HEAD INJURY/TRAFFIC ACCIDENT OR ALTERCATION IN THE PAST 7 HOURS? | | |
| 6. ARE YOU AN ALCOHOLIC?           DATE OF LAST DRINK: HOW MUCH DO YOU DRINK? | | |
| 7. ANY SEIZURES OR DTS? | | |
| 8. DO YOU USE ANY STREET DRUGS SUCH AS HEROIN, COCAINE, METHAPHETAMINE, MARIJUANA OR ANY OTHER DRUGS? | | |
| 9. ARE YOU RECEIVING METHADONE? __DETOX OR __MAINTENANCE | | |
| 10. DO YOU HAVE ANY RASHES, CUTS, BOILS, ABSCESSES, OR OTHER SKIN DISEASES? | | |
| 11. DO YOU HAVE ANY ARTIFICIAL LIMBS, BRACES, DENTURES, HEARING AID, CONTACT LENSES OR EYEGLASSES? | | |
| 12. HAVE YOU EVER TRIED TO HARM YOURSELF OR TAKE YOUR OWN LIFE? WHEN: | | |
| 13. ARE YOU THINKING OF HARMING YOURSELF NOW? | | |
| 14. ARE YOU CURRENTLY RECEIVING PSYCHIATRIC TREATMENT? | | |
| 15. HAVE YOU BEEN A PATIENT IN A HOSPITAL WITHIN THE LAST 3 MONTHS? | | |
| 16. HAVE YOU EVER BEEN TREATED AT A REGIONAL CENTER OR DIAGNOSED WITH DEVELOPMENTAL PROBLEMS? | | |
| 17. DO YOU KNOW OF ANY MEDICAL REASON WHY YOU CANNOT WORK IN JAIL? | | |

| **TRIAGE DISPOSITION** | **WORK STATUS** |
| --- | --- |
| __ACCEPTABLE FOR BOOKING | __GENERAL |
| __MEDICAL | __KITCHEN |
| __REFER TO MENTAL HEALTH | __LITE DUTY/NO KITCHEN |
| __REFUSED ASSESMENT | __NO WORK |
| __E.R. REASON | __HOLD FOR FOLLOW-UP/RECHECK ON: |

# Crime Scene Entry Log Sheet

## ALL PERSONS ENTERING THE CRIME SCENE MUST SIGN THIS SHEET

AGENCY: _____ Case #: _____

SCENE LOCATION: _____

Note: Officers assigned to maintain scene security must also log in and out on this sheet and should state their reason as "Log Officers."

| Name & Title | Signature | Agency | In Date/Time | Out Date/Time | Reason for Entering Scene |
|---|---|---|---|---|---|
| | | | / | / | |
| | | | / | / | |
| | | | / | / | |
| | | | / | / | |
| | | | / | / | |
| | | | / | / | |

Page _____ of _____

# Photography Log Sheet <sub></sub>pg ___ of ____ pgs

AGENCY: _____ Case #: _____

SCENE LOCATION: _____

| Photo # | Evidence Marker # | Description of Evidence Photographed |
|---------|-------------------|--------------------------------------|
|         |                   |                                      |
|         |                   |                                      |
|         |                   |                                      |
|         |                   |                                      |
|         |                   |                                      |
|         |                   |                                      |
|         |                   |                                      |
|         |                   |                                      |
|         |                   |                                      |
|         |                   |                                      |
|         |                   |                                      |

_____  _____  _____  _____

Name & Title          Badge #          Signature             Agency

# Evidence Bag Example

### (Information that should be written on evidence bag.)

///////////////////////////////////////// / Edge of Tape

--------------------------------------------------------------------Edge of bag ( bag opening)

///////////////////////////////////////// Edge of Tape

Case _____

Date _____

Suspect _____

Property Record & Receipt _____

Item _____  _____

Item Description _____

Officer _____

Badge _____

Dept _____

Note: Place your initials across the edge of the evidence tape where it meets the bag/box. Initial at the top, bottom, and side edges of the tape. The purpose of the tape is to detect unauthorized entry. Do not use masking tape. Use evidence tape or wide scotch tape.

# POLICE PROPERTY RECORD & RECEIPT FORM - CHAIN OF CUSTODY

## (α → ∑Δ → Ω)     PRR # _____

| Name of Investigating Officer | Badge Number | Report # / Citation # |
|---|---|---|
| Name of officer submitting evidence to lab | Badge Number | Lab # (issued by lab) |
| Date of Evidence Collection | Time of Evidence Collection | Who was evidence collected from |

| Location of recovery | | County |
|---|---|---|
| Witnesses to recovery | | |
| Specific detail or title of offense (use law book if a crime) | | Offense code (only if criminal case) |

## Evidence Description for Lab (quantity, serial #, identifying marks, color, etc.)

| Item # | |
|---|---|
| Item # | |
| Item # | |
| Item # | |
| Item # | |

## Chain of Custody (If no subjects involved when items recovered, use word "recovered" in "From" box.)

| Item | Date/Time | From: Signature & Badge # | To: Signature & Badge # | Code | Location | Remarks |
|---|---|---|---|---|---|---|
| | | | | | | |
| | | | | | | |
| | | | | | | |
| | | | | | | |
| | | | | | | |

## Code: T = Transferred; S = Stored; R = Released; D = Destroyed

# POLICE PROPERTY RECORD & RECEIPT FORM - CHAIN OF CUSTODY

## (α → ∑Δ → Ω)    PRR # _____

| Name of Investigating Officer | Badge Number | Report # / Citation # |
|---|---|---|
| Name of officer submitting evidence to lab | Badge Number | Lab # (issued by lab) |
| Date of Evidence Collection | Time of Evidence Collection | Who was evidence collected from |

| Location of recovery | County |
|---|---|
| Witnesses to recovery | |
| Specific detail or title of offense (use law book if a crime) | Offense code (only if criminal case) |

## Evidence Description for Lab (quantity, serial #, identifying marks, color, etc.)

| Item # | |
|---|---|
| Item # | |
| Item # | |
| Item # | |
| Item # | |

## Chain of Custody (If no subjects involved when items recovered, use word "recovered" in "From" box.)

| Item | Date/Time | From: Signature & Badge # | To: Signature & Badge # | Code | Location | Remarks |
|---|---|---|---|---|---|---|
| | | | | | | |
| | | | | | | |
| | | | | | | |
| | | | | | | |
| | | | | | | |

Code: T = Transferred; S = Stored; R = Released; D = Destroyed

# REQUEST FOR POLICE LABORATORY EXAMINATION

☐ New Case   ☐ Supplemental Case   Lab Assigned Report # _____

| Name of Investigating Officer | Badge Number | Case # | PRR # |
|---|---|---|---|
| Police Agency & Address | | Phone # | ORI # |
| Date | | Time | County of Occurrence |

| Type of Case Investigation (most serious criminal violation) | Police Case Report # |
|---|---|
| Suspect Name | Victim Name |
| Delivered to lab by / Badge # | Received in lab by / Date & time |

## Evidence Description for Lab (quantity, serial #, identifying marks, color, etc.)

| Item # | Description of Items being submitted to lab |
|---|---|
| | |
| | |
| | |
| | |
| | |
| | |
| | |

Lab Exam Request (Specify each item number to be tested.  For example, state, "Test item X for ……")

_____

_____

_____

_____

# REQUEST FOR POLICE LABORATORY EXAMINATION

☐ New Case     ☐ Supplemental Case     Lab Assigned Report # _____

| Name of Investigating Officer | | Badge Number | Case # | | PRR # |
|---|---|---|---|---|---|
| Police Agency & Address | | | Phone # | | ORI # |
| Date | | | Time | | County of Occurrence |

| Type of Case Investigation (most serious criminal violation) | Police Case Report # |
|---|---|
| Suspect Name | Victim Name |
| Delivered to lab by / Badge # | Received in lab by / Date & time |

## Evidence Description for Lab (quantity, serial #, identifying marks, color, etc.)

| Item # | Description of Items being submitted to lab |
|---|---|
|  |  |
|  |  |
|  |  |
|  |  |
|  |  |
|  |  |
|  |  |

Lab Exam Request (Specify each item number to be tested.  For example, state, "Test item X for ……")

_____

_____

_____

_____

# CERTIFICATE OF PROOF OF CHAIN OF PHYSICAL CUSTODY

(Transfer of evidence from evidence storage to a non-law enforcement party)

_____Police Department     Case _____

Defendant _____


This is to certify that I _____ (name) am employed by

_____ (department)  and that on _____ (date)

I seized from _____ (location or person) pursuant to

_____ (State Whether Subject to a Warrant, Lawful Arrest or Otherwise)

at or near _____(location where items seized)

The following substance(s) or container(s): (Describe substance or container with sufficient particularity to

distinguish it.)

_____

_____

_____

_____

_____

On (date) _____ I made delivery of the above describe items to _____

(person receiving items) with ID _____of (agency) _____ in

substantially the same condition as when I received it.


Place: _____     Date: _____


_____            _____
(Delivering Officer's Signature)            (Receiving Officer's Signature)

# Tape Review Request

_____Police Department

## Communications Bureau

Directions: All requests for reviewing recorded conversations must be authorized by the Communications Supervisor, or his designee.

Conversation Type:   Telephone_____        Radio_____     Video _____

Incident Date: _____ Approximate Time: _____

Agency: _____ Case Number: _____

Complainant: _____

Requesting Officer & Badge #:_____

Reason for Request: _____

_____

_____

_____

_____

Received by:_____Date:_____

Communications Bureau Authorization:_____

# SUBPOENA

| _____ Court | ◊ County    ◊ City   of _____ |
|---|---|
| STATE OF _____<br><br>     vs.<br><br>_____<br><br>_____<br><br>_____ | Cause Number: _____<br><br>Subpoena for (charge title & code):<br><br><br>Charge _____; Code_____ |

To:

**YOU ARE HEREBY COMMANDED** to appear in the above named court at the place, date, and time specified below to testify in the above case.

| Place:<br><br>_____ Court<br><br>_____<br>Court Address<br><br>Ph: _____ | Courtroom:<br><br><br>Date and Time: |
|---|---|

*This subpoena shall remain in effect until you are granted leave to depart by the court or by an officer acting on behalf of the court.*

| _____ Court Judge or Clerk of the _____ Court | Date |
|---|---|
| This subpoena requested by: | |
| This subpoena is based upon application of the:<br><br>◊ State/Plaintiff     ◊ Defendant | Address of requesting Party: |

# IN FIELD SHOW-UP REPORT

## _____ Police Department

CASE NO._____      PRIORITY  __YES  __NO

| OFFENSE | LOCATION OF OCCURRENCE | |
|---------|------------------------|---|
| VICTIM | DATE OF OCCURRENCE | COUNTY |

## ADMONITION OF VICTIMS AND WITNESSES:

It is requested that you look at an individual who has been temporarily detained by police. You are under no obligation to participate. This person may or may not have committed the crime. It is just as important to eliminate innocent persons from suspicion as it is to identify the perpetrator. Do not let handcuffs or police presence influence your decision. Please do not discuss the case with any other witnesses.

BY SIGNING THIS FORM, I AM INDICATING THAT I FULLY UNDERSTAND THE ADMONITION PRESENTED TO ME BY OFFICER_____, REGARDING THE IN FIELD SHOW-UP.

_____     _____   _____
   Printed Name of Witness        Signature of Witness     Date

## IDENTIFICATION:

☐ I CANNOT IDENTIFY THIS INDIVIDUAL AS THE SUSPECT.

☐ I CAN IDENTIFY THIS INDIVIDUAL AS THE SUSPECT.

ADDITIONAL COMMENTS OF VICTIM/WITNESSES: _____

_____

SIGNATURE OF WITNESS: _____ DATE: _____

WITNESSED BY OFFICER: _____ DATE/TIME: _____

LOCATION OF IN FIELD SHOW-UP_____

DATE & TIME OF IN FIELD SHOW-UP_____

NAME AND DOB OF PERSON VIEWED_____

| Officer's Name (printed) | Officer's Signature & Badge # | Date | Approved by Supervisor |
|--------------------------|-------------------------------|------|------------------------|
| | | | ☐ Yes   ☐ No |

181

# PHOTOGRAPIC LINEUP PROCEDURES

A LINE-UP THAT IS SUGGESTIVE IS INADMISSIBLE IN COURT. TO BE SURE YOUR LINEUP IDENTIFICATION WILL NOT BE EXCLUDED AT TRIAL AS UNFAIR, FOLLOW THESE GUIDELINES.

1. THE PHOTOGRAPIC LINEUP MUST CONSIST OF AT LEAST (6) PHOTOGRAPHS.
2. USE ALL COLOR OR ALL BLACK AND WHITE PHOTOGRAPHS, DO NOT MIX.
3. EVERYONE IN THE DISPLAY SHOULD BE OF THE SAME SEX, RACE, APPROXIMATE AGE AND GENERAL FEATURES.
4. TRY TO USE PHOTOGRAPHS OF THE SAME APPROXIMATE SIZE, DEPICTING THE SAME APPROXIMATE SHOTS OF THE FACES (SUCH AS ALL CLOSE UPS OR NOT CLOSE UPS).
5. LABEL EACH PHOTOGRAPH WITH A NUMBER FROM ONE (1) THROUGH SIX (6 ).
6. IF YOU HAVE TWO OR MORE WITNESSES, SEPARATE THEM BEFORE VIEWING THE LINEUP, SO THAT ONE WITNESS DOES NOT IMPROPERLY INFLUENCE ANOTHER WITNESS (THE OPINIONS NEED TO BE INDEPENDENT FROM ONE ANOTHER).
7. READ THE ADMONITION STATEMENT TO THE WITNESS AND HAVE THE WITNESS SIGN THE ADMONITION PART OF THE REPORT.
8. DISPLAY THE PHOTOGRAPHIC LINEUP TO THE WITNESS.
9. IF POSSIBLE, RECORD THE WITNESS' EXACT WORDS, SUCH AS, "MAYBE IT'S HIM", "I GUARANTEE THAT'S HIM."

# PHOTOGRAPHIC LINE-UP

_____ Police Department

CASE NO._____     PRIORITY __YES __NO

| Offense | Code | County |
|---|---|---|
| Location of offense | Victim | Date of occurrence |

## PHOTOGRAPHIC LINE-UP:

ON_____(DATE/TIME),

AT (Location) _____(Victim/Witness )_____

READ THE FOLLOWING ADMONITION, AND THEN ALLOWED TO VIEW THE PHOTOGRAPH LINE-UP

**ADMONITION OF VICTIMS AND WITNESSES:**
It is requested that you look at a group of photographs. You are under no obligation to pick out any photographs. The suspect may or may not be in the photographic line-up. It is just as important to eliminate innocent persons from suspicion as it is to identify the perpetrator. Please do not discuss the photographs with any other witnesses.

I FULLY UNDERSTAND THE ADMONITION PRESENTED TO ME BY OFFICER_____,
REGARDING THE PHOTOGRAPHIC LINE-UP     ☐YES   ☐ NO

_____     _____  _____
Printed Name of Witness            Signature of Witness       Date

IDENTIFICATION:  ☐ I CANNOT MAKE ANY IDENTIFICATION
                 ☐ I CAN IDENTIFY PHOTOGRAPH _____ AS  THE SUSPECT.

STATEMENT OF WITNESS/VICTIM:

_____

_____

_____


SIGNATURE OF WITNESS: _____ DATE: _____

WITNESSED BY OFFICER: _____ DATE/TIME:_____

PHOTOGRAPH _____IS THAT OF: _____

# CITIZEN'S ARREST

ORDER OF ARREST by PRIVATE PERSON

_____ POLICE DEPARTMENT

TO: POLICE

PEOPLE OF THE STATE OF _____

VS.

_____
DEFENDANT

YOU ARE HEREBY REQUESTED TO TAKE INTO CUSTODY THE ABOVE NAMED DEFENDANT WHO I HAVE ARRESTED FOR THE COMMISSION OF A PUBLIC OFFENSE IN MY PRESENCE. I WILL FURTHER, IN THE INTEREST OF JUSTICE, APPEAR AND SWEAR TO A COMPLAINT AGAINST SAID DEFENDANT, AND WILL APPEAR AS A WITNESS FOR THE PEOPLE IN ANY SUBSEQUENT ACTION WHEN MY PRESENCE IS NECESSARY FOR THE PROSECTION OF SAID DEFENDANT.

I UNDERSTAND THAT HAVING STARTED THESE PROCEEDINGS, I MUST FOLLOW THROUGH AS ABOVE STATE, AND IF I DO NOT, I MAY BE BROUGHT INTO COURT BY PROCESS SO THAT THE CASE MAY BE PROPERLY DISPOSED.

DATE_____TIME_____    _____

SIGNATURE OF ARRESTING PARTY

POLICE OFFICER WITNESSES

_____  _____        _____  _____
Signature & Badge          Date               Signature & Badge          Date

# USE OF FORCE REPORT

| INCIDENT INFORMATION | | | | |
|---|---|---|---|---|
| DATE | TIME | LOCATION | COUNTY | CASE # |

| | |
|---|---|
| TYPE OF INCIDENT | ___RESPONDING TO DISTURBANCE/INCLUDING DOMESTIC VIOLENCE<br>___INVESTIGATING/INTERVIEWING SUSPICIOUS PERSON<br>___CIVIL DISORDER           ___ATTEMPTING ARREST<br>___OFFENDER MENTALLY DERANGED   ___BURGLARIES IN PROGRESS<br>___HANDLING OR TRANSPORTING PRISONERS  ___ROBBERIES IN PROGRESS<br>___TRAFFIC STOPS/PURSUITS       ___AMBUSH<br>___ALL OTHER ACTIVITY |

## OFFICER INFORMATION

| NAME | BADGE# | SEX | RACE | AGE | INJURED | YEARS OF SERVICE |
|---|---|---|---|---|---|---|
| | | | | | ☐ YES ☐ NO | ___1-5 ___6-10 ___11-15 ___16-20<br><br>___21-25 ___26-30 ___OVER 30 |

## SUBJECT

| NAME | SEX | RACE | AGE | WEAPON ☐ YES ☐ NO | INJURED ☐ YES ☐ NO | ARRESTED ☐ YES ☐ NO |
|---|---|---|---|---|---|---|
| | | | | | | |

| UNDER THE INFLUENCE (ALCOHOL OR DRUGS)   ☐ YES   ☐ NO | ORIGINAL OFFENSE | CODE |
|---|---|---|

| SUBJECT'S ACTIONS<br>(CHECK ALL THAT APPLY) | OFFICER'S MEANS OF CONTROL<br>(CHECK ALL THAT APPLY) |
|---|---|
| __RESISTED POLICE OFFICER CONTROL<br><br>__PHYSICAL THREAT/ATTACK ON OFFICER OR ANOTHER<br><br>__THREATENED/ATTACKED OFFICER OR ANOTHER WITH BLUNT OBJECT<br><br>__THREATENED/ATTACKED OFFICER OR ANOTHER WITH CUTTING OBJECT<br><br>__THREATENED/ATTACKED OFFICER OR ANOTHER WITH MOTOR VEHICLE<br><br>__THREATENED OFFICER OR ANOTHER WITH FIREARM<br><br>__FIRED AT OFFICER OR ANOTHER<br><br>__ATTEMPTED TO EVADE ARREST BY FLIGHT<br><br>__OTHER (SPECIFY) | __COMPLIANCE HOLD<br><br>__HANDS/FISTS<br><br>__KICKS/FEET<br><br>__CHEMICAL AGENT<br><br>__USE OF BATON OR OTHER OBJECT<br><br>__OTHER (SPECIFY)<br><br>**FIREARMS DISCHARGE**<br><br>___INTENTIONAL<br><br>___ACCIDENTAL<br><br>NUMBER OF SHOTS FIRED_____<br><br>NUMBER OF HITS_____ |

## OTHER OFFICERS ON SCENE

| NAME: | BADGE# | NAME: | BADGE# |
|---|---|---|---|
| | | | |

185

# Use of Firearms Diagram Information

**(e.g., for destruction of deer)**

Not to Scale                                                          N ↑

LOCATION of INCIDENT


Point of Impact (POI)


Measurements from fixed reference point


## *Additional information*

Once the scene is drawn, 4 items that are required on a firearms report are a) location of shooting, b) North, c) not to scale, d) and measurements.

Always make North point upward on the diagram. This will make the report consistent and easier for others to read.

Make sure officer is in safe position relative to deer and traffic (i.e., when traffic is clear, shoot downward toward deer and away from traffic).

Measure all important distances from fixed reference points (points that will not likely move). Do not use the parked police vehicle as the reference point (because it can easily be moved). At a minimum, there should be at least 2 measurements on diagram (x and y coordinates). More measurements result in a more detailed and accurate diagram.

Label all items on the diagram (may label one tree to represent group). Draw and label deer, individuals, and vehicles at scene. Be sure to draw scene so that it indicates that the shooting was performed safely.

# FIREARMS REPORT

## _____ Police Department

| FIREARMS REPORT # | LOCATION OF SHOOTING | | ON DUTY? ☐ YES ☐ NO |
|---|---|---|---|
| DATE & TIME OF SHOOTING | TYPE OF AREA (Rural, Residential, etc.) | | WERE OFFICIAL PHOTOS TAKEN? <br> ☐ YES ☐ NO |
| TYPE OF FIREARM USED | SERIAL NO. OF WEAPON | OWNER OF WEAPON | ISSUED TO |
| OBJECT(S) FIRED UPON | | | NO. OF SHOTS: <br><br> __FIRED __HIT TARGET |
| WITNESS (NAME, ADDRESS, TELEPHONE NO.) | | | |

### SHOOTING INCIDENT (COMPLETE DIAGRAM ON NEXT PAGE)

**Narrative:**

| Officer's Name (printed) | Officer's Signature & Badge # | Date | Approved by Supervisor <br><br> ☐ Yes ☐ No |
|---|---|---|---|

# Firearms Diagram

| Officer's Name (printed) | Officer's Signature & Badge # | Date | Approved by Supervisor |
|---|---|---|---|
| | | | ☐ Yes    ☐ No |

# VEHICLE PURSUIT CRITIQUE FORM

_____*POLICE DEPARTMENT*

INSTRUCTIONS: THIS FORM IS TO BE COMPLETED BY THE FIELD SUPERVISOR WHEN AN OFFICER IS INVOLVED IN A VEHICULAR PURSUIT.

CASE NUMBER:_____ INCIDENT DATE:_____ INCIDENT TIME:_____

| OFFICER(S) INVOLVED | BADGE | UNIT |
|---|---|---|
| INITIATING OFFICER | | |
| BACK-UP OFFICER(S) | | |
| OTHER OFFICER(S) | | |
| APPROVING SUPERVISOR(S): | | |
| OTHER AGENCIES INVOLVED (LIST DEPARTMENTS) | | |

1. WAS THE PURSUIT INITIATED BY THIS AGENCY?  ___YES  ___ NO

2. LOCATION WHERE PURSUIT BEGAN:_____

3. LOCATION WHERE PURSUIT ENDED:_____

4. DID THE PURSUIT LEAVE THE CITY LIMITS?  ___YES  ___ NO

5. DID THE PURSUIT LEAVE COUNTY LIMITS?  ___YES  ___ NO

6. WHAT WAS THE INITIAL VIOLATION COMMITTED?_____

7. WHAT WAS THE REASON FOR THE PURSUIT?  CHECK ALL THAT APPLY.

  A.____ THE IMMEDIATE OR FUTURE DANGER TO THE PUBLIC CREATED BY THE PURSUIT WAS LESS THAN THE IMMEDIATE OR FUTURE DANGER TO THE PUBLIC IF THE SUSPECT OF A VIOLENT CRIME REMAINED AT LARGE.

  B.____ THE SUSPECT OF A VIOLENT CRIME ATTEMPTED TO AVOID DETENTION OR APPREHENSION BY USING HIGH SPEED OR OTHER EVASIVE TACTICS THAT CREATED A DANGER TO THE PUBLIC.

  C.____ THE SUSPECT OF A VIOLENT CRIME FAILED TO YIELD TO THE OFFICER'S VISIBLE & AUDIBLE SIGNAL TO STOP.

  D.____ ASSIST ANOTHER AGENCY (NAME OF AGENCY) _____

8. HOW MANY PUBLIC SAFTEY VEHICLES WERE INVOLVED IN THE PURSUIT?_____

9. WERE ANY UNMARKED UNITS INVOLVED? ___YES ___ NO  HOW MANY?_____

10. WERE ANY ROADBLOCKS USED ___YES ___ NO

11. WERE ANY TIRE DEFLATING DEVICES USED? ___YES ___ NO

12. WERE THERE ANY INJURIES OR FATALITIES? ___YES ___ NO

___OFFICER ___SUSPECT ___ 3$^{RD}$ PARTY

NAME(S):_____

13. WAS ANY PROPERTY OR VEHICLES DAMAGED? ___YES ___ NO

14. RESULT OF PURSUIT: ___TERMINATION ___ ESCAPE ___ TRAFFIC COLLISION ___ ARREST

CHARGE(S)_____

| | |
|---|---|
| **ADMINISTRATIVE REVIEW** | POLICY COMPLIANT? ____YES ____NO<br><br>DEPARTMENT TRAINING ADEQUATE? ___YES ___ NO<br><br>SUPERVISOR _____ DATE_____ |

# Injury Report – Corrections Employee

_____ Department

| Case Report # |
|---|

| Address of Incident: |
|---|

| Name of Officer | Badge # | Date of Incident | Time of Incident | Date of Report |
|---|---|---|---|---|

| On Duty | Location | Type of Assault |
|---|---|---|
| ☐ Yes | ☐ Indoors | ☐ Cut  ☐ Stabbed  ☐ Kicked/Punched  ☐ Shot |
| ☐ No | ☐ Outdoors | ☐ Contaminated with Substance/Fluids  ☐ Other |

| Location of assault on body |
|---|
| ☐ head  ☐ eyes  ☐ mouth  ☐ torso  ☐ legs  ☐ feet  ☐ hands  ☐ other _____ |

| Did Employee Remain on Duty? | Did Employee See Doctor? | Name of Attending Doctor |
|---|---|---|
| ☐ Yes    ☐ No | ☐ Yes    ☐ No | |

| Employee's Statement |
|---|

| Witnesses' Statements |
|---|

| Supervisor's Statement |
|---|

| Supervisor's Name & BADGE # |
|---|

# INMATE VIOLATION REPORT

## _____ Police Department

| Case Report # | | | | |
|---|---|---|---|---|
| **Address of Incident:** | | | | |
| **Name of Inmate** | **Inmate ID #** | **Date of Incident** | **Time of Incident** | **Date of Report** |

| **Injuries Involved** | **Injured (check all that apply)** | **Names of Injured** |
|---|---|---|
| ☐ Yes<br><br>☐ No | ☐ Inmate  ☐ Facility Employee<br><br>☐ Visitor  ☐ Other _____ | 1) _____<br><br>2) _____<br><br>3) _____ |

Types of Treatment for

Injured person # 1 _____

Injured person # 2 _____

Disposition of Injured for

Injured person # 1 _____

Injured person # 2 _____

Recommendation of Corrections Officer

☐ Criminal Charges  ☐ Loss of Privileges  ☐ Loss of Wages  ☐ Other (describe below)

| Employee's Name & Badge # | Supervisor's Name & Badge # |
|---|---|

# Custody Request Form - Detention Division

## _____Police Department

Inmate's Name:_____ Housing Unit:_____

Charges:_____ Code(s)_____

Requesting Officer:_____

Police Agency:_____ Phone:_____

Reason for Custody Request (Check One)

☐ Serve Warrant     ☐ Interview     ☐ Court     ☐Other _____

I will assume responsibility for the safety and security of the above named inmate while he/she is in my custody.

_____          _____
Receiving Officers Signature                                    Date

.......................................................................................................................

## Detention Center Use Only

Date and Time Out_____/_____          Releasing Deputy_____
                                        Badge _____

Date and Time In_____/_____          Receiving Deputy_____
                                        Badge _____

Remarks:_____
_____
_____
_____
_____

# APPLICATION FOR EMERGENCY PROTECTIVE ORDER

_____ Police Department          Case _____

1. PERSON(S) TO BE PROTECTED BY THIS ORDER (insert all names):_____

_____

2. PERSON TO BE RESTRAINED (name):_____

DOB _____ Sex ____ Race ____ Ht ____ WT ____ Hair _____ Eyes _____

Tattoos or marks _____

3. The events that cause the protected person to fear immediate and present danger for self and/or children are described below.

4. ___ The person to be protected lives with the person to be restrained and requests an order that the restrained person move out immediately.

5. ___ The person to be protected has minor children in common with the person to be restrained.

6. ___ A temporary custody order ___ does ___ does not  exist.

7. ___ The person to be protected is a minor child, who is in immediate danger of being abducted by the person to be restrained.

Applicant's Name: _____ Address: _____

Judge: _____ Signature: _____

Court:_____ Telephone No.:_____

# EMERGENCY PROTECTIVE ORDER

Issued by _____ Court _____ County _____ State

Police Case _____ Police Department _____

Persons Protected by Restraining Order _____

_____

**To restrained person (name):** _____

1.  You must not harass, strike, threaten, communicate with, destroy any personal property, or disturb the peace
    of all persons named above.

2. You must stay away at least

____ yards from each person named above

____ yards from address _____

3. You are

____ not required to move out of residence (address) _____

____ immediately required to move out of residence (address): _____

4. _____ (name) is given temporary care and control of the following minor children
of the parties (names and ages): _____

Reasonable grounds for the issuance of this order exist and an emergency protective order is necessary to
prevent the occurrence or recurrence of violence or abuse.

THIS EMERGENCY PROTECTIVE ORDER WILL EXPIRE AT _____ (time) ON: _____ (date)

**PROOF OF SERVICE**

5. Person served (name): _____

6. I personally delivered copies to the person served on  DATE: _____ Time: _____

7. Location Served (address): _____

Name of Server _____ Signature _____

Department _____ Address _____

I declare under penalty of perjury that the foregoing is true and correct.

# DOMESTIC VIOLENCE SUPPLEMENTAL

_____ POLICE DEPARTMENT      CASĚ _____

| VICTIM'S NAME | DOB | OFFENSE | CODE |
|---|---|---|---|
| | | | |

**INITIAL OBSERVATIONS/CRIME DESCRIPTION**

I RESPONDED TO A CALL OF                                AT

I FOUND THE VICTIM (LOCATION):

| CONDITION OF VICTIM | THE VICTIM DISPLAYED THE FOLLOWING EMOTIONAL AND PHYSICAL CONDITIONS: |
|---|---|

| | |
|---|---|
| __ANGRY        __COMP OF PAIN | |
| __APOLOGETIC   __BRUISE(S) | |
| __CRYING       __ABRASION(S) | |
| __FEARFUL      __MINOR CUT(S) | |
| __HYSTERICAL   __LACERATION(S) | |
| __CALM         __FRACTURE(S) | |

| | |
|---|---|
| __AFRAID       __CONCUSSION(S) | SUSPECT'S NAME / DOB |
| __NERVOUS      __THREATENING | |
| __IRRATIONAL   __OTHER EXPLAIN | HOME ADDRESS / PHONE |

| SUSPECT | WORK ADDRESS / PHONE |
|---|---|

| | |
|---|---|
| __ANGRY        __COMP OF PAIN | |
| __APOLOGETIC   __BRUISE(S) | PRIOR HISTORY OF DOMESTIC VIOLENCE?  __YES __NO |
| __CRYING       __ABRASION(S) | |
| __FEARFUL      __MINOR CUT(S) | |
| __HYSTERICAL   __FRACTURE(S) | PRIOR HISTORY OF VIOLENCE DOCUMENTED? __YES __NO |
| __CALM         __LACERATION(S) | |
| __AFRAID       __CONCUSSION(S) | |
| __IRRATIONAL   __OTHER EXPLAIN | NUMBER OF PRIOR INCIDENTS __MINOR __SERIOUS |
| __NERVOUS | |
| __THREATENING | |
| __OTHER EXPLAIN | CASE NUMBER(S)_____ |
| | |
| EXPLAIN _____ | INVESTIGATING AGENCY:_____ |

**RELATIONSHIP BETWEEN VICTIM AND SUBJECT**

**MARK ALL THAT APPLY**

LENGTH OF RELATIONSHIP _____ YEAR(S) _____ MONTH(S)

__SPOUSE        __FORMER SPOUSE        __COHABITANTS        __FORMER COHABITANTS

**IF APPLICABLE,**

__DATING/ENGAGED   __SAME SEX   __FORMER DATING   DATE RELATIONSHIP ENDED _____

__EMANCIPATED MINOR   __PARENT OF CHILD FROM RELATIONSHIP

**EVIDENCE**

| MEDICAL TREATMENT | PARAMEDICS AT SCENE: __YES __NO | HOSPITAL:_____ |
|---|---|---|
| __NONE | UNIT NUMBER:_____ | ATTENDING |
| __WILL SEEK OWN DOCTOR | NAME(S) IĎ _____ | PHYSICIAN(S): _____ |
| __FIRST AID | _____ | _____ |
| __PARAMEDICS | | |
| __HOSPITAL | | _____ |
| __REFUSED MEDICAL AID | | _____ |

**EVIDENCE COLLECTED FROM**

___CRIME SCENE   ___HOSPITAL   ___OTHER (EXPLAIN)

PHOTOS ___YES   ___NO   PHOTO LOG NUMBER: _____

PHOTOS OF VICTIM'S INJURIES ___YES   ___NO

PHOTOS OF SUSPECT' INJURIES ___YES   ___NO

WEAPON USED DURING INCIDENT ___YES   ___NO
TYPE OF WEAPON USED_____

WEAPON(S) IMPOUNDED ___YES   ___NO

FIREARM(S) IMPOUNDED FOR SAFETY ___YES   ___NO

PROPERTY RECORD & RECEIPT (PRR) _____

DESCRIBE ALL EVIDENCE AND ITS DISPOSITION

| Officer's Name (printed) | Officer's Signature & Badge | Date | Approved by Supervisor □ Yes   □ No |
|---|---|---|---|
|  |  |  |  |

# Trespass Warning

_____ Police Department

Case Number _____

(Name)_____ (Race) _____

(Sex)_____ (DOB) _____ (SSN) _____

Was warned   □ by me or   □ in my presence    to stay off the property

at (address) _____


This warning was given on (date) _____ at (time) _____

  By (business/property owner) _____


The above named person was advised that if he/she returns onto
Said property, he/she will be in violation of law and subject to arrest.
There are no time limits for this warning.  The person so warned
was given notice of this warning.


Police Officer (printed name) _____

Police Officer signature _____

Badge# _____

# SUSPECTED CHILD ABUSE REPORT

_____ Police Department   Case _____

| REPORTING PARTY | OFFICER NAME & BADGE | | SIGNATURE | |
|---|---|---|---|---|
| | ADDRESS | PHONE | DATE OF ARREST | |

| REPORT SENT TO | ___POLICE DEPARTMENT   ___SHERIFF'S OFFICE   ___COUNTY WELFARE   ___COUNTY PROBATION | | |
|---|---|---|---|
| | AGENCY | ADDRESS | |
| | OFFICIAL CONTACTED | PHONE | DATE/TIME |

**INVOLVED PARTIES / GUARDIANS/PARENTS/SIBLINGS/VICTIMS**

| NAME OF PERSON WATCHING CHILD | PHONE | DOB | SEX | RACE |
|---|---|---|---|---|

PRESENT LOCATION OF CHILD (ADDRESS)

| NAME | ROLE IN FAMILY | ADDRESS | PHONE | DOB | SEX | RACE |
|---|---|---|---|---|---|---|
| 1. | | | | | | |
| 2. | | | | | | |
| 3. | | | | | | |
| 4. | | | | | | |
| 5. | | | | | | |
| 6. | | | | | | |

**INCIDENT INFORMATION**

| DATE/TIME OF INCIDENT | PLACE OF INCIDENT |
|---|---|

IF CHILD WAS IN OUT-OF-HOME AT THE TIME OF INCIDENT, CHECK TYPE OF CARE:

___FAMILY DAY CARE     ___CHILD CARE CENTER     ___FOSTER FAMILY HOME

___SMALL FAMILY HOME   ___GROUP HOME OR INSTITUTION

TYPE OF ABUSE: (CHECK ONE OR MORE)

___PHYSICAL     ___MENTAL     ___SEXUAL ASSAULT     ___NEGLECT     ___OTHER

NARRATIVE DESCRIPTION:

SUMMARIZE WHAT THE ABUSED CHILD OR PERSON ACCOMPANYING THE CHILD SAID HAPPEN

EXPLAIN KNOWN HISTORY OF SIMILAR INCIDENT(S) FOR THIS CHILD:

# Police Department - Victim's Notification and Wavier

Name of Victim_____ Case # _____ Date _____

_____
Victim Address                                              Home Phone

_____
Place of Work                      Address                  Work Phone

Emergency contact: _____ Phone _____

Name of Suspect:_____ AKA_____

Warrant/Summons Number:_____ County _____

Offense Charged:_____ Code _____

Children Present:_____ Ages:_____

**You are responsible for informing the Police Department and the appropriate court of any changes in your residency, employment, or phone number.**

**As the victim of a criminal offense being investigated by the Police Department:**

I would like to be notified when an arrest has been made in this case:   □ Yes     □ No

**As the victim of a criminal offense (Court Date, if known:_____ )**

I would like to be present when a person arrested in this case appears for a

Bond Hearing:          □ Yes    □ No
Preliminary Hearing:  □ Yes    □ No
Plea:                  □ Yes    □ No
Trial or Sentencing:   □ Yes    □ No

**As the victim of an individual who is being detained in a jail or other detention facility for a criminal offense, I would like to be notified:**

When a person arrested in this case is
released:        □ Yes   □ No
transferred:     □ Yes   □ No
escapes:         □ Yes   □ No

**Waiver:** I fully understand my rights as a victim and do not wish to be notified of any court proceedings:  □ Yes   □ No

_____   _____   _____
Victim's Signature              Date              Officer's Signature & Badge

**For Criminal Domestic Violence Cases Only**

Under provisions of Law, I am advising you of the following information:

1. You have the right to "Petition for an order of Protection" in this incident from the Family Court.

2. If you wish to seek an "Order of Protection" in this incident, you must preserve evidence and/or may need witnesses to assist you in your case. You also may have to testify in court.

3. Do you have an "Order of Protection" from the Family Court?
   ☐ Yes    ☐ No

4. Do you seek protection at this time?
   ☐ Yes    ☐ No

5. Do you need transportation to a shelter or hospital?
   ☐ Yes    ☐ No

6. Do you need an officer to accompany you to your residence to remove personal items?
   ☐ Yes    ☐ No

I acknowledge that the reporting officer has advised me of my rights as a victim in this matter, and I understand them completely.

Victim Signature _____    Date _____

Officer Signature & Badge ____ _____    Date _____

**Victim Rights: As a victim of a crime, you have the following rights and responsibilities.**

To be treated with fairness and dignity, and to be free from intimidation, or harassment, or abuse, throughout the criminal and juvenile justice process.

To be informed of your constitutional rights provided by statute.

To be reasonably informed when the accused or convicted person is arrested, released from custody, or has escaped.

To be reasonably informed of and be allowed to submit either a written or oral statement at all hearings affecting bond or bail.

**Victim Acknowledgement**

As a victim of crime, I have received a copy of the Victim/Witness Rights and Responsibilities sheet provided to me by a Police Officer and I agree that if I should have a change of address, I must notify the appropriate agency in order for Law Enforcement to make a reasonable attempt to contact me for court proceedings and inmate status.

# Wanted/Missing Person Report

| | |
|---|---|
| Case | Police Dept. |
| Officer: | Badge: |

| Wanted/Missing Person | |
|---|---|
| Last Name | First Name |
| Social Security Number | ID (Number & State) |
| DOB | ID (Type) |
| Race/Sex | Skin Tone |
| Height/Weight | Jewelry |
| Eye Color/Hair Color | Clothing Description |
| Blood Type | Emancipation Date |

| |
|---|
| Caution Indicator (If applicable) |

| |
|---|
| Aliases |

| Scars, Marks, Tattoos | **Check One**<br><br>__ Disabled<br>__ Juvenile Runaway<br>__ Crime Victim<br>__ Suspect<br>__ Person of Interest<br>__ Other |
|---|---|

| Vehicle Information | |
|---|---|
| Vehicle License No. & State | Number of Doors |
| VIN | Color/Make/Model |

Comments: _____

I attest to the validity of the above information.

_____

Name(printed)          Signature          Badge          Date

# MISSING CHILD REPORT

_____ Police Department   Case _____

| NAME (LAST, FIRST, MIDDLE) | ALIAS |
|---|---|
| SEX __M __F    RACE __ASIAN __INDIAN __BLACK __WHITE __UNKNOWN | PLACE OF BIRTH (CITY & STATE) |

| DOB | AGE | NAME & ADDRESS OF LAST DAY CARE CENTER |
|---|---|---|

| HT | WT | EYE COLOR __ BROWN __ BLUE __ GREEN __ HAZEL __OTHER_____ | HAIR STYLE __AFRO __CURLY __ BRAIDED __ PONYTAIL __STRAIGHT |
|---|---|---|---|

| HAIR COLOR __ BLACK __ BROWN __ RED __ NO HAIR __ BLONDE __ OTHER _____ | HAIR LENGTH __EAR __SHOULDER __COLLAR __ BELOW SHOULDER __N/A |
|---|---|
| | FACIAL HAIR __ NONE __ UNSHAVEN __ MUSTACHE __ BEARD __ GOATEE |

| SKIN TONE __ FAIR/LIGHT __ MEDIUM __ DARK __BLACK __ RUDDY __OTHER | TEETH __PROTRUDING __ GAPS __ GOLD-CAPPED __ CHIPPED __ DECAYED __ STRAIGHT |
|---|---|
| BUILD __ THIN __ MEDIUM __ HEAVY __MUSCULAR | |

| SCARS, MARKS, TATTOOS, ETC. |
|---|

| SSN | DL | STATE |
|---|---|---|
| DATE & TIME: LAST SEEN | TIME(MILITARY) | LOCATION LAST SEEN |

LAST SEEN WEARING (LIST ALL AVAILABLE DESCRIPTORS:

HOBBIES, INTERESTS, ASSOCIATIONS, HANGOUTS:

POSSIBLE DESTINATION (NAME & LOCATION):

POSSIBLY IN COMPANY WITH (NAME & AGE):

| LICENSE PLATE | STATE | VEHICLE YR | MAKE | MODEL | STYLE | COLOR |
|---|---|---|---|---|---|---|

| CORRECTED VISION __ YES __ NO __ GLASSES __CONTACTS | BLOOD TYPE | MEDICATION REQUIRED (REASON & TYPE) |
|---|---|---|

| JEWELRY TYPE/ DESCRIPTION | INITIAL ASSESSMENT __FAMILY ABDUCTION __NON-FAMILY ABDUCTION __ RUNAWAY        __OTHER_____ |
|---|---|

203

# CRIME SCENE CHECKLIST

_____ POLICE DEPARTMENT   Case _____

| REPORTING OFFICER | | BADGE | | Date | |
|---|---|---|---|---|---|
| CALL TIME | | ARRIVAL TIME | | DEPART TIME | |

## SCENE DESCRIPTION

| | | | | | |
|---|---|---|---|---|---|
| INDOORS | ☐ YES   ☐ NO | FORCED ENTRY | | ☐ YES | ☐ NO |
| RESIDENTIAL | ☐ YES   ☐ NO | HOMEOWNER PRESENT | | ☐ YES | ☐ NO |
| COMMERCIAL | ☐ YES   ☐ NO | BUSINESS OPEN | | ☐ YES | ☐ NO |
| OUTDOORS | ☐ YES   ☐ NO | POINT OF ENTRY | | ☐ YES | ☐ NO |
| VEHICLE | ☐ YES   ☐ NO | MAKE AND MODEL | | ☐ YES | ☐ NO |
| ROADWAY | ☐ YES   ☐ NO | HIGHWAY | | ☐ YES | ☐ NO |
| FIELD | ☐ YES   ☐ NO | TYPE (HAY, COTTON, ETC) | | | |

## SCENE DOCUMENTATION

| | | |
|---|---|---|
| PHOTOS TAKEN ☐ YES ☐ NO | VIDEO TAKEN ☐ YES ☐ NO | SKETCH DONE ☐ YES ☐ NO |

## VICTIM #1: INFORMATION

| NAME | | DOB | AGE | HAIR | EYES |
|---|---|---|---|---|---|
| ADDRESS | | SSN | HT | WT | |

| VICTIM SHOT | ☐ YES   ☐ NO | AREA OF INJURY (HEAD, ARM, ETC) |
|---|---|---|
| DECEASED | ☐ YES   ☐ NO | AMOUNT OF DECOMPOSITION |
| ALIVE | ☐ YES   ☐ NO | APPROX. TIME OF DEATH (HOURS) |
| INJURED | ☐ YES   ☐ NO | WEAPON USED (KNIFE, GUN, ETC.) |

## VICTIM #2: INFORMATION

| NAME | | DOB | AGE | HAIR | EYES |
|---|---|---|---|---|---|
| ADDRESS | | SSN | HT | WT | |

| VICTIM SHOT | ☐ YES   ☐ NO | AREA OF INJURY (HEAD, ARM, ETC) |
|---|---|---|
| DECEASED | ☐ YES   ☐ NO | AMOUNT OF DECOMPOSITION |
| ALIVE | ☐ YES   ☐ NO | APPROX. TIME OF DEATH (HOURS) |
| INJURED | ☐ YES   ☐ NO | WEAPON USED (KNIFE, GUN, ETC.) |

| NAME | | DOB | AGE | HAIR | EYES |
|------|---|-----|-----|------|------|
| ADDRESS | | SSN | HT | WT | |

| WAS SUSPECT ARRESTED? ☐ YES ☐ NO | WAS SUSPECT ARRESTED ON SCENE? ☐ YES ☐ NO |
|---|---|
| SUSPECT CLOTHES COLLECTED?<br>☐ YES ☐ NO | WAS A WEAPON COLLECTED FROM SUSPECT?<br>☐ YES ☐ NO |
| DESCRIPTION OF CLOTHING COLLECTED AS EVIDENCE: | |
| TYPE OF WEAPON COLLECTED FROM SUBJECT OR FROM LOCATION DURING INVESTIGATION | |

## WEAPON INFORMATION: WAS WEAPON COLLECTED?  ☐ YES  ☐ NO

| TYPE (REVOLVER, SEMI AUTO, PISTOL, RIFLE, ETC) | MAKE |
|---|---|
| MODEL | SERIAL |
| CALIBER | TYPE AMMO |
| WHERE WAS WEAPON COLLECTED? | OF NON-SPENT ROUNDS IN CYLINDER |
| | OF SPENT ROUNDS IN CYLINDER |
| WAS WEAPON LOADED?  ☐ YES  ☐ NO | WAS WEAPON STOLEN?  ☐ YES  ☐ NO |

**Draw the cylinder's chambers and the position of each casing.  Label each spent and non-spent round.**

**CYLINDER POSITION**

**EVIDENCE**

| TYPE OF EVIDENCE COLLECTED | | | DESCRIPTION |
|---|---|---|---|
| WEAPON | ☐ YES | ☐ NO | |
| FOOTWEAR/TIRE WEAR | ☐ YES | ☐ NO | |
| LATENT | ☐ YES | ☐ NO | |
| SEROLOGICAL | ☐ YES | ☐ NO | |
| TRACE | ☐ YES | ☐ NO | |
| NARCOTICS | ☐ YES | ☐ NO | |
| OTHER | ☐ YES | ☐ NO | |

| | |
|---|---|
| WAS EVIDENCE PACKAGED AND SEALED? | ☐ YES ☐ NO |
| WERE ITEMS SUBMITTED TO EVIDENCE ROOM? | ☐ YES ☐ NO |

# Stolen Items Notification

## _____ Police Department

| STOLEN | | | |
|---|---|---|---|
| VEHICLE | VEHICLE TAG | GUN | ARTICLE |
| LIC. # | LIC. # | MAKE | TYPE OF ARTICLE |
| LIC. STATE | | | |
| VIN | LIC. STATE | SERIAL # | BRAND NAME |
| MAKE | | | |
| MODEL | OFFICER | CALIBER | MAKE |
| COLOR | | | SERIAL # |
| # DOORS | BADGE # | TYPE OF GUN (Pistol, Rifle, etc.) | |
| MODEL YEAR | | | Owner Applied # |
| DATE OF THEFT | DEPT | | |
| OFFICER | | OFFICER | |
| BADGE # | CASE# | BADGE # | BADGE # |
| DEPT | | DEPT | DEPT |
| CASE# | | CASE# | CASE# |

Comments: _____

I attest to the validity of the above stolen item.

Victim's Printed Name  _____  Date _____

Victim's Signature  _____

Officer Signature & Badge _____  _____  Date _____

# JUVENILE INFORMATION
## TO BE OBTAINED BY POLICE OFFICERS

JUVENILE'S NAME:_____

JUVENILE'S ADDRESS:_____

DOB:_____ SOC. SEC. #_____ ID #:_____ ID Type _____

SCHOOL ATTENDED:_____ GRADE:_____

CUSTODIAL PARENT'S NAME:_____

ADDRESS:_____

HOME PHONE:_____ WORK PHONE:_____

PLACE OF EMPLOYMENT:_____

NON-CUSTODIAL PARENT'S NAME:_____

ADDRESS:_____

HOME PHONE:_____ WORK PHONE:_____

PLACE OF EMPLOYMENT:_____

STEP-PARENT'S NAME:_____

PLACE OF EMPLOYMENT:_____

PRIOR JUVENILE DELINQUENCIES: [LIST YEAR, COUNTY, AND TYPE OF CHARGE]:

_____

COMMENTS BY OFFICER: _____

_____

_____

# Juvenile Notice of Violation

_____ Police Department    Tracking _____

**ATTENTION PARENT/GUARDIAN: YOU AND THE BELOW NAMED JUVENILE WILL BE NOTIFIED BY MAIL WHEN TO REPORT TO THE POLICE PROBATION DEPARTMENT.**

| JUVENILE NAME (LAST, FIRST, MIDDLE) | | | SEX | RACE | DOB | AGE |
|---|---|---|---|---|---|---|
| ADDRESS | | PHONE | SCHOOL | | GRADE | |
| VEHICLE (YR, MAKE, MODEL) | LICENSE | DRV LIC | OTHER ID | | | |
| PARENT/GUARDIAN NAME | ADDRESS | HOME PHONE | WORK PHONE | | | |

| **VIOLATIONS** | DATE | TIME | | |
|---|---|---|---|---|
| STATUTE_____ | LOCATION | | | |
| ORDINANCE_____ | COMPANIONS | | | AGE |
| __CURFEW __POSS ALCOHOL/DRUGS | | | | AGE |
| __WEAPON(S) __DISTURBANCE/ASSAULT | | | | AGE |
| __TRESPASSING/PROWLING __GANG ACTIVITY __VANDALISM | OFFICER'S SIGNATURE | | BADGE | |
| __OTHER_____ | JUVENILE'S SIGNATURE | | | |

| REMARKS: |
|---|
|  |

| CONTACT WITH PARENTS/GUARDIANS  ☐YES  ☐NO | DATE | TIME | OFFICER & BADGE |
|---|---|---|---|
| NAME: | | | |

# RELEASE TO CUSTODY

STATE OF _____     COUNTY OF _____

### IN THE FAMILY COURT

I, _____

Hereby agree to be responsible for my child and to have my child _____ ,

with a DOB of _____ , AVAILABLE AT THE TIME OF HEARING in the

Family Court at such time as the Court may direct, if he/she is released to my custody.

**Failure to comply with this agreement will result in the issuance of an**

**arrest warrant for my arrest.**

□ Mother          □ Father          □ Guardian

_____          _____

Printed Name of Parent or Guardian          Signature of Parent or Guardian

_____

Date

Witnesses: _____          _____

Name & Badge          Name & Badge

# Juvenile Fingerprint Card - Final Disposition

(Below is some information that might be asked for the final disposition that involves a juvenile.)

Original Charge _____ Code _____

Filed Charge _____ Code _____

Amended Charge _____ Code _____

☐ Dismissed    ☐ True    ☐ Not True    ☐ Waived to Adult Court    ☐ Informal Adjustment

DOC Commitment ( da ys) _____    Suspended:    ☐ YES    ☐ NO

Counseling ( da ys) _____

Court Cost _____    Fine _____    Restitution _____

Suspended DL:    ☐ YES    ☐ NO

# APPENDIX

# **GENERAL INFORMATION FOR REPORTS (fictitious)**

## Police Department

1) Aiken City Police Department

   111 Laurens St Aiken, SC 29802

   District 2   ph: 803-555-0911;   ORĬ   00049004400

2) Aiken County Sheriff Office

   2423 Hampton Ave Aiken, SC 29801

   District 43   ph: 803-555-9110;   ORĬ   00390005300

## ORI # s

1) 330053000;   2) 74000543000;   3) 440054000;   4) 8800056000

## Dispatch

1) Badgĕ   394        2) Badgĕ   126        3) Badgĕ   292

## Post Command

1) Badgĕ   1        2) Badgĕ   2            3) Badgĕ   11

## Court Information

1) Aiken County Superior Court        2) Aiken Town Court              3) Aiken Co. Circuit Court

   121 Laurens St Aiken, SC 29802        22 US HWY 1 Aiken, SC 29802        48 Laurens St

   ph: 803-555-1212                      ph: 803-555-5492                    Aiken, SC 29803

                                                                             ph: 803-555-4444

# Vehicles

(Fictitious information; VINS are variables only and may not represent proper format)

1. WASHINGTON, D.C. REGISTRATION

Plate: 8SU95    Expires: 6/1/2017

Yellow 2004 Honda Civic   3 Door

Vehicle No.: JF2HF72J34154930

**2.** NEW JERSEY REGISTRATION

Plate: GD32KH    Expires: 8/5/2018

Purple 2007 Ford F-150    2 Door

Vehicle No.: 1F2HF72J37154930

3. OHIO REGISTRATION

Plate: HAPPY    Expires: 7/4/2017

Red 2003 Volkswagen Jetta    4 Door

Vehicle No.: WF2HF72J33154930

4. MISSOURI REGISTRATION

Plate: ALP138    Expires: 8/5/2019

Green 2001 Hyundai Accent   2 Door

Vehicle No.: KF2HF72J31154930

5. SOUTH CAROLINA REGISTRATION

Plate: 8SU95    Expires: 6/1/2017

Yellow 2004 Ford Mustang   2 Door

Vehicle No.: JF2HF72J34154930

**6.** GEORGIA REGISTRATION

Plate: HJ32HF    Expires: 8/15/2019

Black 2014 Ford Crown Victoria    4 Door

Vehicle No.: 1F2HF72J47199394


7. NORTH CAROLINA REGISTRATION

Plate: TX5728    Expires: 7/4/2019

Yellow 2013 Rolls Royce   Phantom   4 Door

Vehicle No.: WF2HF72J43154544


8. FLORIDA REGISTRATION

Plate: 85H77    Expires: 11/22/2022

White 1986 Chevy Caprice  2 Door

Vehicle No.: KF4HF52J31959432


9. CALIFORNIA REGISTRATION

Plate: CA5714    Expires: 7/4/2017

Orange 2014 BMW  328i  Sedan    4 Door

Vehicle No.: WF2HF72J94154930


10. TEXAS REGISTRATION

Plate: P4489P    Expires: 8/5/2019

Green 1981 Ford Granada   4 Door

Vehicle No.: KF2HF72J81193381


11._____ REGISTRATION

Plate  H3478    Expires: ____

Silver 2014 Honda Accord  2 Door

Vehicle No.: JF2HF72J94361276

# REPORT NUMBERS

Case Report

    1)  C2014-0716-0900

    2)  C2015-0879-3949

    3)  C2016-1111-1930

Incident

    1)  I2014-33304

    2)  I2015-57476

    3)  I2016-1212-120

Property Record & Receipt

    1)  PRR 4959

    2)  PRR 2912

    3)  PRR 3X23

Crash Report

    1)  76-2014-0711-013

    2)  44-2015-0831-303

    3)  11-2015-1111-202

Firearm Report

    1)  FAR2014-33

    2)  FAR2015-41

Mug

    1)  AA-4082

    2)  BB-30003

    3)  CC-4948

# Drivers/Suspects/Victims/Witnesses (fictitious)

1) Jacquelyn D.  LoGiudice  dob= 7-19-1992  b/f/5-0/95/brn/blue;  SSN = 000-88-3321

2) James S. King dob= 3-6-1980  w/m/6-1/211/brn/haz/tattoo: skull on F/R shoulder; SSN = 000-44-1441

3) Phillip D. Carl dob=9-11-1957  b/m/6-0/195/brn/brn; SSN = 000-76-3021

4) Heather D. Danielle  dob=7-23-1993  a/f/5-1/100/red/blu; SSN = 000-19-3042

5) Ashley D. Brooke dob=9-17-1994  b/f/5-7/140/brn/brn; SSN = 000-34-3234

6) Juan Gonzalas dob= 5-8-1988 h/m/5-8/177  brn/brn; tattoo:marijuana leaf L-forearm; SSN = 000-91-3948

7) Olga E. Hernandez dob=11-15-1977 h/f/5-0/110/brn/brn/tattoo:"O" on back of neck; SSN = 000-11-2038

8) Brandon A. McHenry  dob=10-01-2000  b/m/5-8/155/bln/blu; SSN = 000-21-7673

9) Gina F. Fortuna dob=2-28-1982  w/f/5-3/110/bln/brn; SSN=000-77-8959

10) Angela Davis   dob=10-17-1936  w/f/4-10/121/brn/grn; SSN = 000-10-1936

11) Glenn D. Dean  dob=11-7-1960  b/m/5-8/180/brn/hazel; SSN = 000-12-1023

12) David C. Lee   dob=08-31-1966  w/m/5-4/140/bln/brn; SSN = 000-65-7798

# ID #s  (fictitious)

1) SC   473832044

2) MI   D203291020

3) TN   4939393

4) OH   48293675

5) Ontario (Canada)   5R40G368

6) MO   5838320

7) NJ   5905030

8) DC   6849309

9) MO   48943832

10) GA   58949839

# DL #s  (fictitious)

1) AK  H583359

2) DC  5737203

3) RI  G35128H2

4) MA  583894939

5) Puerto Rico  P76774R

6) OH  5949309

7) MO  K58398

8) OR  F683932

9) TX  T472829

10) FL  5738202

11) GA  48393298

12) KY  5839209

13) NC  N583929

14) NJ  583302

15) CA  4829292

16) SC  49209277

17) MI  D411529

# Phone #s  (fictitious)

1) ph: 260-555-3392

2) ph: 803-555-2935

3) ph: 313-555-5948

4) ph: 410-555-0932

5) ph: 503-555-1199

# Address/Roadway Locations (fictitious)

1) 1134 Laurens St Aiken, SC 29801

2) 3374 Sims Street Graniteville, SC 29829

3) 34 Laurens St  Aiken, SC 29801

4) 1203 US HWY 1 Graniteville, SC 29829

5) 48 Wall Lake Orland, MO 63005

6) 4900 Avondale Greenville, SC  29602

7) 9450 Tin Lane  Alpine,  NJ 07620

8) 1121 Lincoln Ave Ashley, SC 29821

9) 23947 Richland Ave Aiken, SC 29801

10) US HWY 1 at Sudow Lake Rd (EB) (Graniteville, SC)

11) 2276 US HWY 1 Graniteville, SC 29829

12) 2276 US HWY 1 Graniteville, SC 29829 Parking Lot 5

13) I-20 MP 11 (WB) (Aiken, SC)

14) I-20 MP 22 (EB) (Aiken, SC)

15) Laurens St south of Richland Ave (SB)  (Aiken, SC)

16) Pine Tree road at Maple Tree Ave (SB) Burnettown, SC 29829

17) Kalamazoo Lane south of Battle Ax Ave (EB) Warrenville, SC 29828

18) 483 N 102 E  Washington, DC 20001

19) 4838 Simms Ave  Augusta, GA 30912

20) 5783 Washington Street  Augusta, GA 30912

21) 538 Green Street  Westland, MI 48185

22) 11969 Fourth Street  Marion, NC 28752

23) 244 Starr Ave  Sunbury, OH 43074

# Insurance Information (fictitious)

1) Insurance Co. Progressive; policy 3834704

   Agent: T.A. Marakus  ph: 800-555-2944

2) Insurance Co. Traveler's; policy T4929Y 2

   Agent: Templeton Smith  ph: 800-555-5383

3) Insurance Co. Nationwide; policy NW 3829265

   Agent: Jennifer Armstrong   ph: 800-555-9090

4) Insurance Co. State Farm; policy 3834704

   Agent: Kirk Allen  ph: 800-555-3214

5) Insurance Co. All State; policy 3834704

   Agent: Tiffany Jones   ph: 800-555-4444

# County of Residence

1) Wayne

2) Cass

3) Aiken

4) Lexington

5) Lagrange

6) Richland

7) Elkhart

# Tractors

1) Kenworth 2010 Conventional; VIN 1K24321490J48734

   OH Registration XC3821; expires 12/21/2020


2) Peterbuilt 2013 Cab Over; VIN 1P283424733H41123

   MI Registration AB4396; expires 2/15/2019


3) Freightliner 2014 Conventional; VIN 1F28574824G03495

   MO Registration B58311; expires 07/17/2021


# Trailers

1) Strick 2011 Box; VIN 1S77621491J54134

   NJ Registration TC4832; expires 11/11/2020


2) Talbert 2012 Flatbed; VIN 1T237524723H44443

   IN Registration AB4923; expires 12/05/2021


3) Dorsey 2013 Box; VIN 1D22121823G03275

   CA Registration C38243; expires 08/27/2022

# Exercises

## Daily Activity Report

Today you wrote 25 citations; you changed one flat tire for a driver; you obtained 33 completed traffic dispositions from the courthouse; you gave two Alco-sensor tests (.03% BAC & .26% BrAC); you gave one DataMaster test (.25% BrAC); you made one DUI arrest (felony); you investigated one crash and issued one citation during the crash investigation (expired DL); you went to traffic court for 1 hour during your shift; and you gave 7 warnings total.

Shift: 8:00 am - 7:00 pm; (your shift included ½ hour lunch break & 2 hours overtime for seatbelt patrol)

Entire shift mileage: 50,403 - 50,693;   Seatbelt patrol mileage: 50, 655 - 50, 693

Breakdown of the 25 citations:

19 citations to cars; 5 citations to tractor-trailers; 1 citation for public intoxication (no vehicle)

| 19 citations to cars | 5 citations to tractor-trailers |
|---|---|
| 8 for excessive speed | 3 for excessive speed |
| 3 for following too close | 1 for running lights violation |
| 2 adult seatbelt violations | 1 possession of police radio (case 2014-0110-102) |
| 2 child restraint violations | |
| 1 broken taillight | |
| 1 expired driver's license (given at crash) | |
| 1 driving with a suspended driver's license (misdemeanor) | |
| 1 DUI citation (felony) | |

Breakdown of the 7 warnings:

5 warnings to cars; 2 warnings to tractor-trailers

| 5 warnings to cars | 2 warnings to tractor-trailers |
|---|---|
| 3 for excessive speed | 2 for excessive speed |
| 1 seatbelt violation | |
| 1 child restraint violation warning | |

221

# PURPOSE OF REPORTS

Match report with its purpose


____ To remove the vehicle from the scene

____ Provides free fuel to drivers

____ To collect suspicious criminal activity, but do not have PC for an arrest

____ Involves chain-of-custody

____ Form used to record when a police officer changes a tire for a driver

____ A criminal charge filed by a police officer

____ Includes field sobriety test results

____ Report that records damage to vehicles

____ A report of criminal activity when PC exists

____ Form used to record a high school anti-drug speech


A) Crash Report

B) Public Speaker –Community Relations Form

C) Salvation Army Voucher

D) Police Service Report

E) Information

F) Vehicle Impound Form

G) DUI PC Affidavit

H) Case Report

I) Intelligence Report

J) Property Record & Receipt Form

# Crash: Collision vs. Non-Collision

Check the appropriate box.

Remember, **collisions may involve "other participants".**

| | Indicate type of crash. Each incident sustained some sort of damaged to vehicle or injury to person. | Collision | Non-collision |
|---|---|---|---|
| 1 | A car backs into another car. | | |
| 2 | Car turns too fast and rolls over. There is much damage to car. | | |
| 3 | Semi tanker leaks hazardous material onto parking lot surface at gas station. | | |
| 4 | Car hits traffic sign. Sign is damaged; no damage to car. | | |
| 5 | Flood waters cover car. | | |
| 6 | Hail hits car and causes dents. | | |
| 7 | Man stands on motorcycle and falls off. Man hurt; no damage to motorcycle. | | |
| 8 | A tractor-trailer stops too fast and the cargo shifts, which damages the wall of the trailer. | | |
| 9 | A brake fire expands and consumes a tractor. | | |
| 10 | A rock flies from the tire of a truck and cracks the windshield of a car. | | |
| 11 | A tractor trailer jackknifed and damaged its trailer. | | |
| 12 | A u-joint on the drive shaft breaks and the drive shaft bounces off of the ground and damages the undercarriage of the car. | | |
| 13 | As a vehicle approaches a bridge, a suspect throws a brick from the bridge and the brick hits the vehicle's windshield, which damages the windshield. | | |
| 14 | A car slides off of the roadway and hit a pile of snow/ice in the median, which damages the front of the vehicle. | | |
| 15 | A person shoots a car as it passes and the bullet shatters the passenger side window. | | |

# SCENARIOS

# Citation and Warning

**You work at Aiken City Police Department; District 22  ORI # 23294844;  Badge No. 1342**

**Initial Contact: You observe and stop car for speeding and following too close at 8:30 am on today's date: US Hwy 1 at Flute Ave (EB) Aiken, SC in Aiken County**

Driver: James Ward  dob= 1-13-73 w/m/5-8/190/blu/bln

Address: 2055 Wallace St Aiken, SC 29803

OLN = SC   3745637  (regular DL)

**Vehicle:**        Washington, D.C. REGISTRATION

   Plate:  88X95    Expires: 7/1/2019

   Yellow 2004 Honda    2 Door

   Vehicle No.: 1F2HF72J34154930

**Write Citation** for following too close

**Write Warning** for speed

Directions: use Aiken City Court  111 Anywhere St Aiken, SC 29801   (803)555-1217;

Provide 30 day notice to respond

# Citation & Warning

## 1) Write citation for running red light

## 2) Write warning for speed (68MPH in 55 MPH zone)

You work for Aiken County Sheriff Office, Traffic Division,  Badge 393 4

Aiken County Sheriff Office  3848 Walton Avenue  Aiken, SC 29801  ph: (803)555-1825

Court Information:  Aiken Superior Court 1212 Laurens St  Aiken, SC 29801

(803)555-1373;  Traffic Court date = last Wednesday of Month 9:00 am

Use current date and time

Offense  Location: US HWY 1 at Sudow Lake Rd (EB)   (Graniteville City in Aiken County)

Driver 1: person 3; DL 3; address 3;     Owner of V1:  same as D1

**V1  South Carolina** REGISTRATION

   Plate: GH323N    Expires: 9/5/2022

   Red 2009 Hyundai Accent    2 Door

   Vehicle No.: 1F2HF72J399783709

Insurance: All State policy   AS58374;      Agent: Matthew Murdock  ph: 803-555-1313

# Case Report

## Complete a case report

You work at Aiken County Police Department 123 Yale Ave, Aiken, SC 29802

District 44   ph: 803-555-1316   ORI # 23251114

Post Command Badge No. 5450

Use current date and time.  You stop the vehicle described below at 2276 US HWY 1 in Graniteville, SC for speed (30 MPH in a 15 MPH zone).  The vehicle has two occupants. You smell what appears to be marijuana.  You ask the driver to open the ash tray and the driver complies, and you see what appears to be marijuana in the ash tray.  You ask the driver what it is and the driver states that it is marijuana. You ask the passenger if it is also hers and she states that it is not hers because she has her own, which she pulls out of her purse and shows you.  You use the NIK Presumptive Drug Test Kit and perform a field test, which indicates positive for marijuana on both samples.

Case # 2015-0501-11711

PRR # 4132 (use sequential numbers as needed)

 MUG # BB-2320 (use sequential numbers as needed)

Use King Wench to tow vehicle:   979 Laurens St in Aiken (803-555-9201)

**Vehicle:**     OH REGISTRATION (owned by driver)

Plate:  OH4894    Expires: 6/30/2019

Yellow 2004 Honda    2 Door

Vehicle No.: 1F2HF72J34154930

2031 Buckeye Lane  Fremont, OH 43420

**Driver:**   From information provided in the Appendix, use person  2, DL  6 , address  18 , phone  1,   Police Dept. = 1, Dispatch = 1, Post Command = 1, Court = 1.

**Passenger**: Use person  1, ID  10, address  20, phone  2

226

# Crash Report

## Complete a crash report.

Crash Location: **2276 US Hwy 1  Graniteville, SC 29829 Parking Lot 8**

Use today's date and time.     Dent to front left fender of car.  Crack in wall/barrier.

D1 stated that the he was EB in parking lot 8 and turned right into the loading dock when he collided with the wall.  The front left of V1 hit the wall.  D1 stated that the passenger's Samsung Galaxy S4 phone that fell off of the center console and broke during the crash. This was corroborated by the passenger. Serial   47322002.  Cost of phone = $99.

Passenger (front seat):  Passenger 1 stated that she has been living with driver since Jan 2012.

Passenger 1 stated that she hurt her neck but that she does not want any treatment.

Use the following information obtained from the Appendix.

Crash report  1

Use Vehicle Registration 6

Driver 1: person 3, DL 16, address 9, phone  2, b usiness phone  3, c ounty of residence 3, insurance 1

Passenger 1: person 9, DL 12, phone  3

Owner of vehicle = same as Driver 1

# Vehicle Crash Proof of Insurance

**Use the information below.  Complete Vehicle Crash Proof of Insurance form for D1/V1.**

One vehicle crash.  Driver 1 has a sore neck.  No one dead.

You work for Aiken County Sheriff Office, Traffic Division, Badge 3934    ph: (803)555-1825

Use current date

Crash Report  201 4-1014-140          Notified 9:02 am  Arrived 9:24 am

Location: I-20 MP 10 WB (11 miles NW of Graniteville, SC)

## Vehicle at Fault

**V1   South Carolina** REGISTRATION

   Plate: GH323N     Expires: 9/5/2021

   Red 2009 Hyundai Accent    2 Door

   Vehicle No.: 1F2HF72J399783709

Driver 1: person 3; DL 3; address 3

Owner of V1:   same as D1

Insurance: All State policy   AS58374;      Agent: Tim Murdock   ph: 803-555-1313

# Personal Illness

## Complete a Police Employee Personal Illness Report.

You work for Aiken County Sheriff Office, Traffic District, Badge 3934    ph: (803)555-1825

Aiken County Sheriff Office  3848 Hampton Avenue  Aiken, SC 29801

You were supposed to work yesterday from 8:00 am – 5:00 pm today.  You called in sick at 4:00 am prior to your shift.

You stayed at home.  You did not go to the doctor.

You only missed one day.  You have returned to work today at 8:00 am.

# Abandoned Vehicle

## Complete an Abandoned Vehicle Form.

You work for Aiken County Sheriff Office, Traffic District, Badge 3934    ph: (803)555-1825

Aiken County Sheriff Office  3848 Hampton Avenue  Aiken, SC 29801

Use current date and time

**V1  Colorado** REGISTRATION

Plate: CA3843   Expires: 1/7/2022

Red 2010 Ford F150   2 Door

Vehicle No.: 1F2HF72J305123215

# Public Speaker

**Complete a Public Speaker – Community Relations Form.**

South Aiken High School requests that you give a talk about saying "no" to drugs.  You gave the talk yesterday at 8:30 am.

South Aiken High School address:  232 East Pine Log Road  Aiken, SC 29803

There is a classroom of students.   You talk for about 20 minutes, and you pass out a brochure to each student called,  *It's called Dope for a reason.*

The teacher stated that she would like you to talk about youth services and traffic safety in the future.

# Police Service Report

**Complete a Police Service Report.**

**Use current date and time.  Driver 11, DL 17, address 21**

**You are on duty and you see a car with a flat tire.  You change the tire.**

**Location:  I-20 MP 21 WB**

**Michigan** REGISTRATION

Plate: IRICH     Expires: 9/5/2021

Red 2006   Ford Mustang    2 Door

Vehicle No.: 1F2HF72J858304372

Driver: SSN 100-45-4953; ph: 583-555-3042

# Permit for Possession of Deer

**Give a Permit for Possession of Deer to the driver from the Police Service Report.** You shot and destroyed a wounded button buck at I-20 MP 21 in the south ditch.

# Salvation Army Voucher

**Complete a Salvation Army Voucher.**

The driver to whom you provided the deer permit has just run out of gas. Provide him fuel.

Department Authorization : AC SO384

Location: I-20 MP 21 WB

Michigan REGISTRATION

    Plate: H84812   Expires: 9/5/2020

    Red 2006  Ford Mustang  2 Door

    Vehicle No.: 1F2HF72J858304372

    Driver: SSN 100-45-4953; ph: 583-555-3042

**Provided fuel at:**
Marathon Station
3523 Sheldon Rd
Graniteville, SC 29802

**Merchant HQ Address**
Marathon Station
1231 Money Lane
Columbia, SC 29814

# CRASH DIAGRAM

Vehicle 1 was traveling on I-26 MP 11 (NB) in the driving lane and collided with a deer head-on.  The deer came out of the east ditch.

**Draw a crash diagram.**  Place the 5 items on the crash diagram that every crash diagram must have on it.  In addition, complete the lines of travel and vehicle direction/labels.  In other words, make the vehicle and directional lines look right.

# DUI: Probable Cause Affidavit

## Complete a DUI Probable Cause Affidavit.

You are investigating a vehicle crash at I-20 MP 16 EB in Aiken, SC. The driver stated that she has a sore neck but she refuses any medical attention. During the crash investigation, you notice empty beer cans in the vehicle. You also smell a strong odor of an alcoholic beverage on the driver's breath. The driver stated that she had a few drinks a couple of hours ago. She stated that there was no passenger with her. You run her record and discover that she has been arrested last month by the Ohio Highway Patrol in Erie County for DUI. You give the driver an Alco-sensor test at 9:56 am and the result was 0.11% BAC.

Suspect SSN 000-54-5663

HI REGISTRATION

Kim, Roger

465 S. King St, RM 102

Honolulu, HI 95813

Plate: T472L    Expires: 7/4/2021

Red 1980 Ford  Granada  4 Door

Vehicle No.: 1F2HF72J30154930

Crash  201 7-1129-2342;  Use Aiken Superior Court

Time notified:  9:31 am;   Time arrived:  9:44 am, current date

Post command badge 3 234;   ORI = 00076001400

DataMaster  = 1938934;   Result = .13 BrAC at 11:59 am.

Location of DataMaster = Aiken County Dept. of Public Safety

James Nibert (223), a certified DataMaster operator, provided you the results.

# REFERENCES

Adams, W. (1999). The interpermeation of self and world: Empirical research, existential phenomenology, and transpersonal psychology. *Journal of Phenomenological Psychology, 30*(2), 39-65.

American Psychological Association. (2010). *Publication manual of the American Psychological Association* (6th ed.). Washington, DC: Author.

Bank, S. (2001). From mental health professional to expert witness: testifying in court. *New Directions for Mental health Services, 91,* 57-66.

Being an effective witness (2001). *Labor Relations Bulletin, 726,* 1-3.

Boccaccini, M. (2002). What do we really know about witness preparation. *Behavioral Sciences and the Law, 20*(1/2), 161-189.

Carter, D. (2002). *Issues in police-community relations: Taken from The Police and the community* (7th ed.). Boston, MA: Pearson Custom Publishing.

Crandall, C., Silvia, P., N'Gbala, A., Tsang, J., & Dawson, K. (2007). Balance theory, unit relations, and attribution: the underlying integrity of heiderian theory. *Review of General Psychology, 11*(1), 12-30.

Defoe, T. (2007). The truth is, you gave a lousy talk. *Chronicle of Higher Education, 54*(17), C1-C4.

Fears, D. (2008, June 12). New criminal record: 7.2 million. *The Washington Post.* Retrieved from http://www.washingtonpost.com/wp-dyn/content/article/2008/06/11/AR2008061103458.html

Federal Bureau of Investigation (2013). *FBI releases 2012 crime statistics.* Retrieved from http://www.fbi.gov/news/pressrel/press-releases/fbi-releases-2012-crime-statistics

Field, A. (2005). *Discovering statistics using SPSS* (2nd ed.). Thousand Oaks, CA: Sage Publications.

Gelo, O., Braakmann, D., & Benetka, G. (2008). Quantitative and qualitative research: Beyond the debate. *Integrative Psychological & Behavioral Science, 42*(3), 266-290. doi:10.1007/s12124-008-9078-3

Hatch, J. (2002). *Doing qualitative research in education settings.* Albany, NY: State University of New York Press.

Huesmann, L.R., & Eron, L.D. (1992). Childhood aggression and adult criminality. In J. McCord (Ed.), *Facts, frameworks, and forecasts: Advances in criminology theory* (p. 137-156). New Brunswick, NJ: Transaction Publishers.

Huesmann, L.R., Eron, L.D., & Dubow, E.F. (2002). Childhood predictors of adult criminality: Are all risk factors reflected in childhood aggressiveness? *Criminal Behaviour and Mental Health*, 12(3), 185-208.

Kelley, L., Mueller, D., & Hemmens, C. (2004). To punish or rehabilitate revisited: An analysis of the purpose/goals of state correctional statutes, 1991-2002. *Criminal Justice Studies*, *17*(4), 333-351.

Kentner, K. (2012). *The Ice Cream Murders: Correlation vs. Causation*. Retrieved from http://biojournalism.com/2012/08/correlation-vs-causation/

Kingsbury, K. (2006). The next crime wave. *Time, 168*(24), 70-77.

Klimon, E. (1985). "Do you swear to tell the truth?" *Nursing Economics, 3*(2), 98-102.

Lambert, D. (2008). *Body language 101: The ultimate guide to knowing when people are lying, how they are feeling, what they are thinking, and more*. Ney York, NY: Skyhorse.

Leedy, P., and Ormrod, J. (2005). *Practical research: Planning and design* (8th ed.). Upper Saddle River, NJ: Pearson Merrill Prentice Hall.

Lewis, D. (2001). *The police officer in the courtroom*. Springfield, IL: Charles C Thomas Publisher, LTD.

LexisNexis (2005). *Immigration law handbook*. Longwood, FL: Gould.

Liptak, A. (2008, April 23). U.S. prison population dwarfs that of other nations. *International Herald Tribune*. Retrieved from http://www.iht.com/articles/2008/04/23/america/23prison.php

Maxey, C., and O'Connor, K. (2007). Dealing with blunders. *T+D, 61*(3), 78-79.

McCarthy, K. (2009). *Growth in prison and jail populations slowing: 16 states report declines in the number of prisoners*. Retrieved from Bureau of Justice Statistics Web site: http://bjs .ojp.usdoj.gov/index.cfm?ty=pbdetail&iid=361

Miller-Johnson, S., Moore, B.L., Underwood, M.K., Moore, B.L., & Cole, J.D. (2005). African-American girls and physical aggression: Does stability of childhood aggression predict later negative outcomes? In D. Pepler, K. Madsen, C. Webster, & K. Levene (Eds.), *The development and treatment of girlhood aggression* (p. 75-101). Mahwah, NJ: Lawrence Erlbaum Associates Publishers.

Navarro, J. (2004). Testifying in the theater of the courtroom. *FBI Law Enforcement Bulletin, 73*(9), 26-30.

Peterson, R. (1954). I swear to tell. *Saturday Evening Post, 227*(10), 88.

Ponterotto, J. (2005). Qualitative research in counseling psychology: A primer on research paradigms and philosophy of science. *Journal of Counseling Psychology, 52*(2), 126-136.

Reardon, K. (1981). *Persuasion: Theory and context.* Beverly Hills, CA: Sage Publications.

Resnick, P. and Knoll, J. (2007). Being an effective psychiatric expert witness. *Psychiatric Times, 24*(6).

Reynolds, D. (1990). *The truth, the whole truth and nothing but...* Springfield, IL: Charles C Thomas Publisher, LTD.

Routledge, F. (2007). Exploring the use of feminist philosophy within nursing research to enhance post-positivist methodologies in the study of cardiovascular health. *Nursing Philosophy, 8*(4), 278-290. doi:10.1111/j.1466-769X.2007.00324.x

Schiappa, E. (1991). *Protagoras and logos.* Columbia, SC: University of South Carolina Press.

Shields, L. (2007). Falsification. *Pediatric Nursing, 19*(7), 37.

Smith, R., & Hilderbrand, D. (n.d.). *Courtroom testimony techniques: Success instead of survival.* Retrieved from http://www.ronsmithandassociates.com/ CTT.htm

Smith, S., Eggen, M., & St. Andre, R. (2006). *A transition to advanced mathematics* (6th ed.). Belmont, CA: Thomson Brooks/Cole.

Speaking successfully (2006) *Techniques: Connecting Educations & Careers, 81*(8), 10-11.

Stewart, S. (2007). *Effective courtroom performance by Indiana law enforcement.* Retrieved from http://www.clarkprosecutor.org

Stremler, F. (1982). *Introduction to communication systems* (2nd ed.). Reading, MA: Addison-Wesley Publishing Company.

Tower, W. (2011). Courtroom demeanor. *Kidjacked.* Retrieved from http://kidjacked.com/ defense/courtroom_demeanor.asp

Tucker, J., Donovan, D., and Marlatt, G. (Eds.). (1999). *Changing additive behavior: Bridging clinical and public health strategies.* New York: Guilford Press.

U.S. Department of Justice (2002). *I-94 Arrival/departure record*. Washington, DC: U.S. Government Printing Officer

U.S. Department of Justice (1991). *I-94W Nonimmigrant visa waiver arrival/departure form*. Washington, DC: U.S. Government Printing Officer

Verma, S. (2005). *The little book of scientific principles, theories, & things*. New York, NY: Sterling.

Wakefield, J. (1995). When an irresistible epistemology meets an immovable ontology *Social Work Research, 19*(1).

Weber, R. (2004). The rhetoric of positivism versus interpretivism: A personal view. *MIS Quarterly, 28*(1), iii-xii.